SharePoint Search Quer

Mikael Svenson

ISBN-13: 978-1505887037

ISBN-10: 1505887038

Acknowledgements

To my loving wife Hege for her understanding and support of my community escapades with SharePoint. Without you I would never have been able to travel around and spread the gospel of SharePoint and search.

To Xander for constantly interrupting me from spending too much time at the computer while being at home. I *do* understand that a 5 year old needs his sword and axe practice, and that moms just don't cut it.

To Puzzlepart for allowing me to have the best job in the world, and for letting me work with such a talented group of people. Without all your crazy questions much of this book would not have been possible.

Table of Contents

Introduction

After I wrote *Working with Microsoft FAST Search Server 2010 for SharePoint* back in 2011/2012 I wowed to never again write a book. Not that I didn't enjoy it, because I did so tremendously, but because it was a lot of work which ate up two vacations and lots of evenings and weekends to complete.

Back in March 2014 I started a blog series named the same as this book as I pretty much had the content ready in my mind and needed to write it out. In December 2014 I wrote the 12th post in the series, ending a seven month writing journey on SharePoint search queries. During this time I also created a speaking session on the same material. During the break after presenting the session I was asked the question: *"Is there a book out there I can read about this stuff?"* The answer then was no.

The answer now is yes! This book is a compilation of those twelve blog posts with some additional edits. I hope you enjoy the result, even though you can read it for free on my blog or at IT Unity, and I hope it may serve as a digital reference in your quest for excellent search.

PS! This book does not cover search schemas, custom full-text indexes or rank profiles, and it helps to have some understanding of how list columns map to crawled properties, and how crawled properties map to managed properties, and the different settings on a managed property.

May the Search be with you! - Mikael Svenson

Chapter 1

KQL Basics

SharePoint 2013/Online comes with two query languages which can be used to formulate your search queries. The Keyword Query Language (KQL) and the FAST Query Language (FQL). KQL is the topic for the first two chapters, and is the query language you will mostly use when writing search queries. KQL is also the query language used in search boxes in SharePoint. FQL is a more technical language and have some extended capabilities over KQL, but most queries can be written or formulated using KQL. FQL is also trickier to execute using the UI/CSOM/REST, but more on that in Chapter 10.

The basis of KQL is a set of operators and special characters you can use to formulate your queries. The KQL version included in SharePoint 2013/Online also have some enhancements over the 2010 version of KQL, brought over from FQL. This chapter will focus on the basic KQL operators and capabilities, while Chapter 2 will expand on some of the new operators available (NEAR, ONEAR, XRANK) and discuss how to craft more complex queries.

Keyword Operators

Keyword operators are what you will use the most as an end-user formulating a query in a search box. Most people will only use variants of the top two, perhaps venturing into phrase searches and property searches.

In order to use a managed property in a full-text query the crawled property must be included in the full-text index or the managed property it is mapped to must be marked as *Searchable* in the search schema.

Note: Search terms entered are case-insensitive but the operators must be in uppercase.

Operator	**Usage**	**Example**
termA termB *Free text query*	One or more terms entered after each other with an implicit AND between each term	A search for *Swedish meatballs* returns only items that have *Swedish* and *meatballs* somewhere in them but not necessarily together.
AND/+ *Boolean AND operator*	This is the default operator and need not be specified. It sets the query to return only items with termA and TermB in them.	Swedish AND meatballs and Swedish +meatballs and Swedish meatballs are essentially the same query.

"termA termB" *Double quotation marks*	Placing double quotation marks around a multiple-term query makes the query a phrase search - only items that match the terms together in an exact phrase are returned.	Searching for "*Swedish meatballs*" returns only items with *Swedish* and *meatballs* together. The terms must follow each other exactly and in the specified order.
OR *Boolean OR operator*	This is the disjunct operator and specifies that matching either of the terms on either side of this operator will satisfy the query. That is, items with either *termA* or *TermB* are returned.	Searching for *Swedish OR meatballs* returns any item with the term *Swedish* in it and any item with the term *meatballs* in it.

NOT/- *NOT operator*	This is the negation operator; it sets a trailing term to be an exclusion query. That is, any item that contains this term is excluded from the result set.	Searching for *Swedish NOT meatballs* returns items that match *Swedish* but no items with the term *meatballs* in them are returned. *Swedish – Meatballs* is essentially the same query.
* *Prefix matching wildcard (postfix is not supported)*	The wildcard operator can be added to the end of partial words to match terms with 0 or more trailing characters. Essentially, all terms starting with the entered characters up to the wildcard are matched.	Searching for *Swed* Meat** matches *Swedish meatballs, Sweden meatballs, Sweden Meatloaf, Swedish Meat,* and so on. These terms are not necessarily together. Phrase search is not supported with wildcards in KQL.

WORDS(termA , termB) *or* ANY(termA termB) *Synonym operator*	The synonym operator allows you to specify terms that should be considered synonyms of each other in the query. *TermA* and *TermB* should be considered to have the same meaning and, therefore, be searched for. This is equivalent to using the OR operator between *termA* an d *termB*. This operator cannot be used with property queries.	Searching for *WORDS(Swedish, Svensk)* returns all items with the term *Swedish* and all items with the term *Svensk*. The difference between *WORDS* and *ANY* is that with *ANY* the terms are ranked as if they were the same term and not by their individual weight. An item with one instance of *Swedish* and two instances of *Svensk* would rank the same as an item with three instances of *Swedish*.

ALL(termA termB) *Boolean AND operator*	Enclosing terms with the *ALL* operator is the same as writing the terms with a boolean *AND* between them. This operator cannot be used with property queries.	Searching for *ALL(Swedish meatballs)* returns only items with *Swedish* and *meatballs* together.

() *Parenthesis*	Parenthesis are used to enclose and isolate a specific part of a complex query. If an opening parenthesis is used, a closing parenthesis must be provided.	*Meatballs NOT (Danish OR Norwegian)*represents a query where all items with the term *meatballs* returns as long as the terms *Danish* or *Norwegian* are not also present. Parenthesis can also be nested. *(Danish OR (Norwegian AND Swedish)) NOT (meatballs OR sausage)* represent a query where items containing either *Danish* or *Norwegian* together with *Swedish,* but not *meatballs* or *sausage.*

Property Queries and Operators

It is important to note that the property restriction cannot include whitespace between the property name, the property operator, and the property value. If a space is encountered, the query is treated as a free-text query. Property restrictions are also limited to a maximum of 2,048 characters. The maximum query length using the SharePoint search front end is also 2,048 characters. Programmatic executions of queries are by default limited to 4,096 characters, with a max limit of 20,480 characters adjustable on the SSA if you are on-premises.

In order to use a managed property in a property restriction the managed property must be marked as *Queryable* in the search schema.

Date properties have a resolution of a full day in KQL, and any hours you enter into the comparisons will be ignored. If you need a more granular resolution on dates see Chapter 10 about using FQL.

Operator	**Supported Managed Property types**	**Example**
= *Equals*	Text, DateTime, Integer, Decimal, Double, YesNo	fileextension:docx
: *Contains*	Text, DateTime, Integer, Decimal, Double, YesNo	author:mikael author:"mikael svenson"
< *Less than*		write<03/27/2014

> Greater than	DateTime, Integer, Decimal, Double	write>03/27/2014
<= *Less than or equal*	DateTime, Integer, Decimal, Double	size<=1000000
>= *Greater than or equal*	DateTime, Integer, Decimal, Double	size>=1000000
<> *Does not equal*	Text, DateTime, Integer, Decimal, Double, YesNo	write<>03/27/2014
.. *Range*	DateTime, Integer, Decimal, Double	size:2000..3000 is equal to size>=2000 AND size<=3000

If two property restrictions with the same property is added to a query, then an *OR* is performed between them, and not the implicit *AND* which is used by default with all other terms.

If the property value contains a hyphen (-) together with the property operator equals (=) or not-equals (<>), then the query itself will not work due a present bug in SharePoint search. As a workaround use contains (:) instead when you have a value with a hyphen.

Author="Jones-Smith" does not include *Jones-Smith* as you would expect, while *Author:"Jones-Smith"* will. The above contains example will however also match *Jones-Smith-Smythe,* as contains matches anywhere in a string.

Examples

Description	Example
Items where the author is either *mikael* or *garth*	author:mikael author:garth
Items where the author is *mikael* and *garth* in the same item	author:mikael AND author:garth
Items where the content type is *Document* and author is *mikael*	spcontenttype:document author:mikael

Property Queries and date intervals

In addition to specifying the date manually in a property query you can use some nifty built-in variables. These variables also work in SharePoint 2010.

Interval	Description	Example
today	Represents the time from the beginning of the current day until the end of the current day.	write=today

yesterday	Represents the time from the beginning of the day until the end of the day that precedes the current day.	write=yesterday
this week	Represents the time from the beginning of the current week until the end of the current week. The culture in which the query text was formulated is taken into account to determine the first day of the week.	write<"this week"
this month	Represents the time from the beginning of the current month until the end of the current month.	write<"this month"
last month	Represents the entire month that precedes the current month.	write: "last month"
this year	Represents the time from the beginning of the current year until the end of the current year.	write<"this year"
last year	Represents the entire year that precedes the current year.	write>"last year"

Query for managed metadata or terms

The clue to query against managed metadata is to make sure your list columns are defined as site columns. By using site columns you get an automatically created managed property for the column which you can query against. The name of the managed property is *owstaxIdColumnName,* where *ColumnName* is the internal name of your list column. For example if you have a site column named *Location* tied to a term set you will have a corresponding managed property to query against named *owstaxIdLocation.*

Note: All site columns will have automatic managed properties assigned to them. By using the automatically created managed properties you save yourself the work of creating new managed properties with the right crawled property mappings.

You can use either the **label** or the **unique identifier** for the term when querying. If you however want to query on a terms children you have to use a different notation as seen in the table below.

Description	**Example**
To query for all items that are tagged with a term It is also possible to query against the term default label as well	GP0 | #<guid>
To query for all items that are tagged with a child of term *The term itself is NOT included in the results*	GPP | #<guid>

To query for all items that are tagged with a term from a term set	GTSet|#<guid>

If you query against the managed property *owstaxIdTaxKeyword* (Enterprise Keywords), taxonomy hierarchies *(GPP/GTSet)* will not work, only the individual term *(GP0)*.

When querying against managed metadata you will use contains (:) instead of equals (=) as the managed property contains a string with both labels and GUIDs, and as such using an exact match will not work.

owstaxId columns are by default included in the full-text index (while other automatic managed properties are not), which means if you query for a term GUID or term set GUID as free text without a property filter, you will get all items tagged with that term/term set regardless of the column they are used in.

Examples

Given the following taxonomy let's show some examples on how you can formulate your queries.

World (fc01ae6d-8ed3-4872-9cef-d2199d52d61c)

India (c8a43f13-5ea1-45f2-b46d-3a1986a1cbd7)
Mumbai (ad491ed9-c21c-46d9-896c-c0d148957c60)
Delhi (c195b6e0-9062-446a-9af1-8ec1a642fede)
France (17587ed2-8433-45a4-9f4b-6825164fcd09)
Paris (01031cfe-2492-47f1-8723-45c63ef70ec9)
Lyon (3b2137a9-3c3a-4676-a50a-14f72ab29175)

Description	Example
All restaurants in Mumbai	owstaxIdLocation:"GP0 | #ad491ed9-c21c-46d9-896c-c0d148957c60" or owstaxIdLocation:"Mumbai"
All restaurants in the World	owstaxIdLocation:"GTSet | #fc01ae6d-8ed3-4872-9cef-d2199d52d61c"
All restaurants in India	owstaxIdLocation:"GPP | #c8a43f13-5ea1-45f2-b46d-3a1986a1cbd7"
All restaurants in India, including India itself	owstaxIdLocation:"GPP | #c8a43f13-5ea1-45f2-b46d-3a1986a1cbd7" AND owstaxIdLocation:"GP0 | #c8a43f13-5ea1-45f2-b46d-3a1986a1cbd7"

All restaurants which has a tagged location	owstaxIdLocation:"GTSet | #fc01ae6d-8ed3-4872-9cef-d2199d52d61c"
All items not tagged from a term set in a list	-owstaxIdLocation:"GTSet | #fc01ae6d-8ed3-4872-9cef-d2199d52d61c" contentclass:STS_ListItem ListID:72b79215-34e1-43fc-8cd5-16d594872aeb *The clue is to add enough including terms to what you want, and then exclude the taxonomy column based on the term set id.*
Boost restaurants tagged with Delhi, if the users location is Delhi, and also boost restaurants which are not tagged at all	(({searchTerms}) {?XRANK(cb=1) owstaxIdLocation:{User.SPS-Location}}) {?XRANK(cb=1) -owstaxIdLocation:"GTSet | #fc01ae6d-8ed3-4872-9cef-d2199d52d61c"} *See Chapter 2 for more information on using XRANK*

Summary

By acquainting yourself with the KQL syntax and how data is stored in SharePoint, you can craft queries for just about anything. Sometimes you have to think about what to exclude instead of what to include, as seen in the managed metadata examples. You might find it easier to write down in a sentence/paragraph what you want to accomplish, and then break down each part of the text into a KQL query, which is then assembled back into the final query using parenthesis to group the parts.

References

Keyword Query Language (KQL) syntax reference
http://msdn.microsoft.com/library/ee558911(v=office.15)

[MS-KQL]: Keyword Query Language Structure Protocol
http://msdn.microsoft.com/en-us/library/hh644280(v=office.12).aspx

Automatically created managed properties in SharePoint Server 2013
http://technet.microsoft.com/en-us/library/jj613136%28v=office.15%29.aspx

Chapter 2

KQL Advanced

Chapter 1 covered the basic query operators of KQL. This chapter will cover the more advanced operators, as well as show examples of how KQL can be put together in useful scenarios with some nice to know managed properties.

Note: Search terms entered are case-insensitive but the operators must be in uppercase.

Operator	Usage	Example
NEAR *NEAR operator*	Specifies that terms in the query must appear within a specific distance or tokens where the operator takes two or more terms and a numeric value to specify the distance *N*. The default numeric value is 8. *<expression> NEAR(n=4) <expression>* or	Searching for *recipe NEAR(3) meatballs NEAR(2) Swedish* returns items where the term *recipe* is within 3 terms of *meatballs*. And the term *meatballs* is within 2 terms of *Swedish*. OK: This is a recipe of tasty Swedish Meatballs FAIL: A Swedish cook creates tasty meatballs from an old family recipe

	<expression> NEAR(n) <expression>	
ONEAR *Ordered NEAR*	Ordered variant of the NEAR operator, where the terms must appear in the specified order. The default numeric value is 8. <expression> ONEAR(n=4) <expression> or <expression> ONEAR(n) <expression>	Searching for *recipe ONEAR(3)meatballs ONEAR(2) Swedish* returns items where the term *recipe* is within 3 terms of *meatballs.* And the term *meatballs* is within 2 terms of *Swedish.* The terms are also in the order: *recipe, meatballs, Swedish.* OK: A recipe for good meatballs comes from Swedish people FAIL: Show me a recipe for Swedish meatballs

XRANK *XRANK rank modifying operator*	XRANK allows for modification of the ranking values in the result set based on an expression and a boost value. XRANK can be applied against both the full-text index and managed properties. The queries take the following format. *<match expression> XRANK(cb=100, rb=0.4, pb=0.4, avgb=0.4, stdb=0.4, nb=0.4, n=200) <rank expression>*	Searching for *Swedish meatballs XRANK(nb=0.5) spicy* returns all items with *Swedish* and *meatballs* and give a normalized boost to any item by 0.5 with the term *spicy* in it.

Important: Pay attention to the use of decimal separators in XRANK queries (or other numeric queries) as the parsing of the decimal separator differs in different locales. Some countries use punctuation and some use comma. To ensure proper parsing regardless of the local of the user executing a query use exponential notation. *0.5* is written as *5E-1, 0.25* as *25E-2,* and *0.025* as *25E-3.*

The XRANK operator can take seven different parameters. As noted on MSDN (http://msdn.microsoft.com/EN-US/library/office/ee558911(v=office.15).aspx#kql_operators), you will typically only use the normalized boost parameter (*nb*) as this parameter provides the necessary control to promote or demote a particular item, without taking standard deviation into account. If you are using the Dynamic Ordering capabilities of the Query Builder, you will see it uses a combination of Constant Boost (*cb*) and Standard Deviation Boost (*stdb*). I have found cases where *nb* don't give any value at all, so using *cb* with *stdb* might be a better approach.

The only way to get XRANK statements working is by trying out different values, and try it out on real data. For real life scenarios this means testing out query boosts on production data. Using the SharePoint 2013 Query Tool is an excellent way to get started to look at the rank values per item and how rank is affected when you change the XRANK parameter values.

Parenthesis can be used to group together different parts of a query as shown in Chapter 1, and may be used on either side of an operator (*AND, OR, NOT, NEAR, ONEAR, XRANK*). You can also nest groups of parenthesis.

Examples

Example 1 - The query below will match items which include either *Swedish* or *Norwegian* together with both *meat* and *sheep,* without having the term *awful* in them. In addition the items have to be last modified within the past year. Items which contain *Michelin* guide in the title will be promoted by 0.5 rank points. Items which contain the term *fish,* will be promoted by 0.1 rank points. Items which have both *Michelin* guide in the title and contain *fish* will in total get 0.6 rank points added.
((((ANY(Swedish Norwegian) AND (meat sheep)) XRANK(cb=0.5) title:"Michelin guide") write: "last year") XRANK(cb=0.1) fish) -awful

Example 2 - The query below will match items of the *Document* content type which are Excel files.
SPContentType:Document fileextension:xlsx

Example 3 - The query below will match items with the term *finance* in documents which are either Word documents or PowerPoint presentation.
finance fileextension:doc fileextension:docx fileextension:xls fileextension:xlsx

Example 4 - The query below will match web sites, lists, libraries and folders which have the term *secret* in the name.
IsContainer:1 secret

Example 5 - The query below will match files which have the term *secret* in the name.
IsDocument:1 secret

Example 6 - List only documents store in OneDrive libraries.
IsMyDocuments:1

Example 7 - List all documents from a specific library or list, limited on the id of list.
ListId:18D36608-943C-4173-8770-589ABBC5B786

Summary

The new operators NEAR, ONEAR and XRANK gives some powerful new features to fine tune what you are matching and how you want results ranked. Also using the *IsContainer, IsDocument* and *IsMyDocuments* managed properties can save you some time when writing queries. Try out the samples to familiarize yourself with how they work, and keep them handy the next time a more complex search challenge arise.

References

Keyword Query Language (KQL) syntax reference
http://msdn.microsoft.com/library/ee558911(v=office.15)

[MS-KQL]: Keyword Query Language Structure Protocol
http://msdn.microsoft.com/en-us/library/hh644280(v=office.12).aspx

SharePoint 2013 Query Tool
https://sp2013searchtool.codeplex.com/

Chapter 3

Query Variables

The basis for query transformations in Result Sources, Query Rules and in search web parts is to write KQL queries. Doing so dynamically is a big bonus. This is where *Query Variables* come into play. Knowing KQL syntax and variable usage will enable you to craft a query for just about anything - as long as you also know the managed properties to query.

As an example the Local SharePoint Results result source is defined with the following query template: *{?{searchTerms} -ContentClass=urn:content-class:SPSPeople}*

The variable parts are the ones enclosed with braces *{}*. *{searchTerms}* will for example be substituted with the query terms used. If you search for *author:"mikael svenson"* the final query sent to the search engine will be expanded to *author:"mikael svenson" -ContentClass=urn:content-class:SPSPeople*

As for the *{?..}* notation enclosing the full statement, this means that if the variables inside this statement are blank or empty then everything between *{?* and the matching end brace *}* will be omitted from the expanded query. If an empty query comes in, the final query is blank and not *-ContentClass=urn:content-class:SPSPeople* as everything is removed due to *{searchTerms}* being empty. This is a very powerful and important notation to know.

Tip: Use *{?..}* around any variable which might be empty to ensure a valid query syntax.

The TechNet article *Query variables in SharePoint Server 2013* lists all the out of the box variables available to you. And there are quite a few of them. Below you will see the variables and expanded sample values for each variable.

Note: The exact definitions for the variables can be found at TechNet (*http://technet.microsoft.com/en-us/library/jj683123.aspx*).

Site and site collection variables

This group of query variables are context aware to the current site or site collection at the URL you are currently viewing or executing a query against. It's important to note that they use the Site/SiteCollection notation and not Site/Web as is the programmatically equivalent also used in managed property names.

Query variable	Examples
{Site} or {Site.URL}	http://intranet.contoso.com/sites/it/phone http://intranet.contoso.com/sites/it
{Site.ID}	The GUID for the site: 8740ca76-da13-474b-9389-0f56bf3e69de
{Site.LCID}	1033 (=English) 1044(=Norwegian)
{Site.Locale}	en-US no-NB

{Site.<property>}	Any property from the property bag of an SPWeb object. {Site.vti_defaultlanguage} return the default locale of the site, same as {Site.Locale}
{SiteCollection} or {SiteCollection.URL}	http://intranet.contoso.com/ http://intranet.contoso.com/sites/it
{SiteCollection.ID} *This is NOT the site collection GUID, but the GUID of the root site*	The GUID for the site collections root site: 0dc39501-02df-47f9-bc9d-351024a93a74
{SiteCollection.LCID}	1033 (=English) 1044(=Norwegian)
{SiteCollection.Locale}	en-US no-NB
{SiteCollection.<property>}	Any property from the property bag of the root site of the site collection {SiteCollection.taxonomyhiddenlist} returns the GUID of the hidden taxonomy list

Page, URL token, query string and request variables

These variables are context aware to the current page's properties or the URL you are using.

Query variable	Examples
{Page} or {Page.URL}	http://intranet.contoso.com/sites/it/phone/SitePages/lumia.aspx
{Page.UsageAnalyticsId}	The GUID for the site: 8740ca76-da13-474b-9389-0f56bf3e69de
{Page.<FieldName>}	Any property/column from the page. {Page.Author} return the Created by user e.g. "Mikael Svenson" {Page.Editor} return the Last modified by user e.g. "John Doe"
{URLToken.<integer>}	For the URL https://intranet/testsite1/SitePages/search.aspx {URLToken.1} = search.aspx {URLToken.2} = SitePages {URLToken.3} = testsite1

{QueryString.<Parameter Name>}	For the URL https://intranet/testsite1/SitePages/search.aspx?ItemNumer=567 {QueryString.ItemNumber} = 567
{Request.<PropertyName>}	I have only managed to get {Request.Url) and {Request.RawUrl} to return values. {Request.RawUrl} return the full URL including query string parameters while {Request.Url} return the URL without query string parameters. MSDN HttpRequest property reference

User variables

Any property available on a user's profile is retrievable via the {User.} variable prefix.

Query variable	Examples
{User} or {User.Name}	John Doe
{User.Email}	john@contoso.com
{User.SID}	SID of the user who issued the query (have not gotten this to work)
{User.LCID}	1033
{User.PreferredContentLanguage}	-1 if not set
{User.PreferredDisplayLanguage}	1033
{User.<property>}	{User.WorkPhone} will return the phone number of a user, and {User.SPS-Interests} will return the interests filled out by the user. Also see the {|...} multi-value expansion later in this chapter.

Term and term set variables

The term variables are related to navigation in SharePoint which is using the term store. In addition they work for item properties which are taxonomy columns.

Query variable	**Examples**
{Term} or {Term.ID} or {Term.IDNoChildren}	GUID of current site navigation node with a prefix of #0 – for example, #083e99dcb-7907-4dc9-abc8-b5614a284f1c. This value can be used to query content of the managed property *owstaxIdMetadataAllTagsInfo* or *owstaxIdProductCatalogItemCatego ry* in a Product Catalog Site Collection, or any other taxonomy based managed property owstaxId*SiteColumnName*

{Term.IDWithChildren}	GUID of current site navigation node with a prefix of # – for example, #83e99dcb-7907-4dc9-abc8-b5614a284f1c. This will return all items tagged with the current site navigation term, or children of the current site navigation term. This value can be used to query content of the managed property *owstaxIdProductCatalogItemCategory* in a Product Catalog Site Collection, or any other taxonomy based managed property owstaxId*SiteColumnName* This value cannot be used to query the content of the managed property *owstaxIdMetadataAllTagsInfo*.
{Term.Name}	The label of the term, for example Blue
{Term.<property>}	Any property from the property bag of the term, including custom properties.
{TermSet} or {TermSet.ID}	GUID of the term set used for current site navigation.
{TermSet.Name}	Label of the term set used for current site navigation.

List and list item variables

List variables are useful when you add search based content on a list view or on an item page. An item page can also be a wiki page or a publishing page.

Query variable	Example
{List}	https://contoso.com/sites/pub/Documents
{List.<property>}	Any property of the current list (but I have only gotten ID and Title to return a value) {List.ID} return the GUID of the list {List.Title} return the name of the list
{ListItem}	URL of the current list item. https://contoso.com/sites/pub/Pages/ArticleTest.aspx

{ListItem.<property>} {ListItem.<tax> .<property>}	Property is internal column name. {ListItem.ID} - 3 {ListItem.Title} - My Title {ListItem.author} - Mikael Svenson If you have a column named Comments {ListItem.Comments} - This is a comment If you have a taxonomy column named TaxCol {ListItem.TaxCol.IDWithChildren}

Other variables

Query variable	Examples
{Today+/- <integer value for number of days>}	{Today} - 2014-04-26 {Today+10} - 2014-05-06 {Today-365} - 2013-04-26
{SearchBoxQuery}	The query value entered into a search box on a page.
{CurrentDisplayLanguage}	en-US
{CurrentDisplayLCID}	1033

Custom query variables

Using custom development (server-side object model) you can insert custom variables to be used in your queries as well as the default ones. Look at the MSDN reference for User Segmentation (*http://msdn.microsoft.com/en-us/library/office/jj870831(v=office.15).aspx*) to get an overview on how to do this, or check out my code from SPC12 (*http://bit.ly/1BcA47k*) where I add information about who you follow into variables *{FollowedUsers}* and *{FollowedSites}*, which are both multi-value variables.

If you want to add custom variables in SharePoint Online, you will have to resort to JavaScript trickery which briefly will be touched on in Chapter 9 about context triggering of query rules.

Variables with spaces or special characters in the values

Values which have spaces or special characters in them will be expanded with quotation marks around them.

author:{User.Name} expands to *author:"Mikael Svenson"*. If you don't want to enclose the value in quotation marks you can escape the variable with *{*.

author:{\User.Name} expands to *author:Mikael Svenson* which would match an *Author* named *Mikael*, and any content including *Svenson*.

Query variables with multiple values

Query variables can contain multiple values, and uses the *{|* syntax:

{|ManagedProperty:{QueryVariable}} or *{|{QueryVariable}}*

The expansion will be made using the *OR* operator, and there is no option for an *AND* expansion. If a user has set the *Ask me about* field on the user profile to: *SharePoint, Search* and *Apps,* then the transformation *{|{User.SPS-Responsibility.Name}}* expands into *((SharePoint) OR (Search) OR (Apps))*.

Examples

Example 1 - The query below will only show AllItems.aspx results for the current site's default Document library. Note the quotes around the full statement and escaping of the variable.	
Query	path:"{\Site.URL}/Forms/Pages/Forms/AllItems.aspx"
Result	path:"https://sharepoint.com/sites/pub/Forms/Pages/Forms/AllItems.aspx"

Example 2 - On a page, show all other pages (omit self) in the same library tagged with term or child term on a taxonomy column named *Category*.	
Query using ID	owstaxIdCategory:{ListItem.Category.IDWithChildren} ListID:{List.ID} -ListItemID:{ListItem.ID} or owstaxIdCategory:{Page.Category.IDWithChildren} ListID:{List.ID} -ListItemID:{ListItem.ID}
Result	owstaxIdTestCategory:#649bf5dc-b26d-4e63-8c97-43967f08f516 ListID:0c8e9283-ded5-4d4f-bd51-152283a67944 -listitemid:3
Query using path	owstaxIdCategory:{ListItem.Category.IDWithChildren} path:"{\Site.URL}/Pages/" -path:{Page.Url}
Result	owstaxIdCategory:#649bf5dc-b26d-4e63-8c97-43967f08f516 path:"https://sharepoint.com/sites/pub/Pages/" -path:"https://sharepoint.com/sites/pub/Pages/ArticleTest.aspx"

Example 3 - On a page, show all other pages in the farm tagged with term or child term on a taxonomy column named Category, and boost equal items with a custom factor from the custom property on the term used. If there is no priority property on the term used, the XRANK part is omitted.	
Query	owstaxIdTestCategory:{ListItem.TestCategory.ID WithChildren} {?XRANK(cb={ListItem.TestCategory.Priority}) owstaxIdTestCategory:{ListItem.TestCategory}}
Result	owstaxIdTestCategory:#649bf5dc-b26d-4e63-8c97-43967f08f516 XRANK(cb=1) owstaxIdTestCategory:#0649bf5dc-b26d-4e63-8c97-43967f08f516

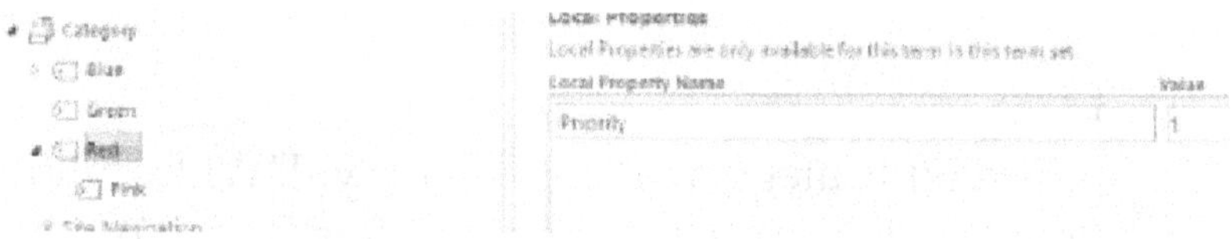

Example 4 - Show items tagged with the same tag as a user's *ask me about* fields. I'm using the general catch all taxonomy column here, but you can use any custom taxonomy column. I have also added {?…} which would remove the query if the user has no values in that field.	
Query	{?{|owstaxidmetadataalltagsinfo:{User.SPS-Responsibility}}}
Result	((owstaxidmetadataalltagsinfo:#00cf9414f-84e4-40ff-8cd7-d3e0a5170887) OR (owstaxidmetadataalltagsinfo:#00b88c4ac-8318-4b3f-b6db-2b2e208fc21c) OR (owstaxidmetadataalltagsinfo:#03da2996f-902d-46b9-96a9-610fd848adc7))

Example 5 - Find items which title contains values from a user's ask me about profile field	
Query	{|title:{User.SPS-Responsibility.Name}}
Result	((title:SharePoint) OR (title:Search) OR (title:Apps))

Example 6 - Pass in a value from the URL query parameter foo. http://contoso.com/Pages/Article.aspx?foo=bar	
Query	title:{QueryString.foo}
Result	title:bar

Example 7 - Pass in a value from the URL query parameter foo. http://contoso.com/Pages/Article.aspx?foo=bar bar	
Query	title:{QueryString.foo}
Result	title:"bar bar"

Summary

Query variables enable you to write re-usable queries using user context or page context to plug in variable or dynamic parts of a query. The ones you will use most often are probably site and site collection ones to scope results to parts of a SharePoint hierarchy, or metadata from a page to bring in relevant content.

References

Query variables in SharePoint Server 2013
http://technet.microsoft.com/en-us/library/jj683123.aspx

MSDN reference for User Segmentation
http://msdn.microsoft.com/en-us/library/office/jj870831(v=office.15).aspx

Custom query variable code from SPC192 - SPC12
https://spsearchparts.codeplex.com/SourceControl/latest#2013/SearchExtension/CustomSearchWebPart/CustomSearchWebPart.cs

Chapter 4

Result Sources

Result sources are one of the key concepts when it comes to SharePoint search, and they are key to deciding where and how a search query is to be executed. If you have previously worked with SharePoint 2010 search, start thinking about scopes and you should be on the right track. But result sources are so much more.

Result sources are used to target specific search indexes. It be the local SharePoint index, an external 2013 farm/SharePoint Online (hybrid scenarios) or an external source via OpenSearch. Result sources may also be used for query transformations, for example to limit results to a particular content type, which is what scopes in 2010 typically was used for.

Note: Result sources are also used to execute searches against Exchange in eDiscovery scenarios.

Limiting/scoping a query is not all a result source can do. A result source can also expand the query using any KQL syntax or query variable, and it can be used to specify how you want results to be sorted or ranked.

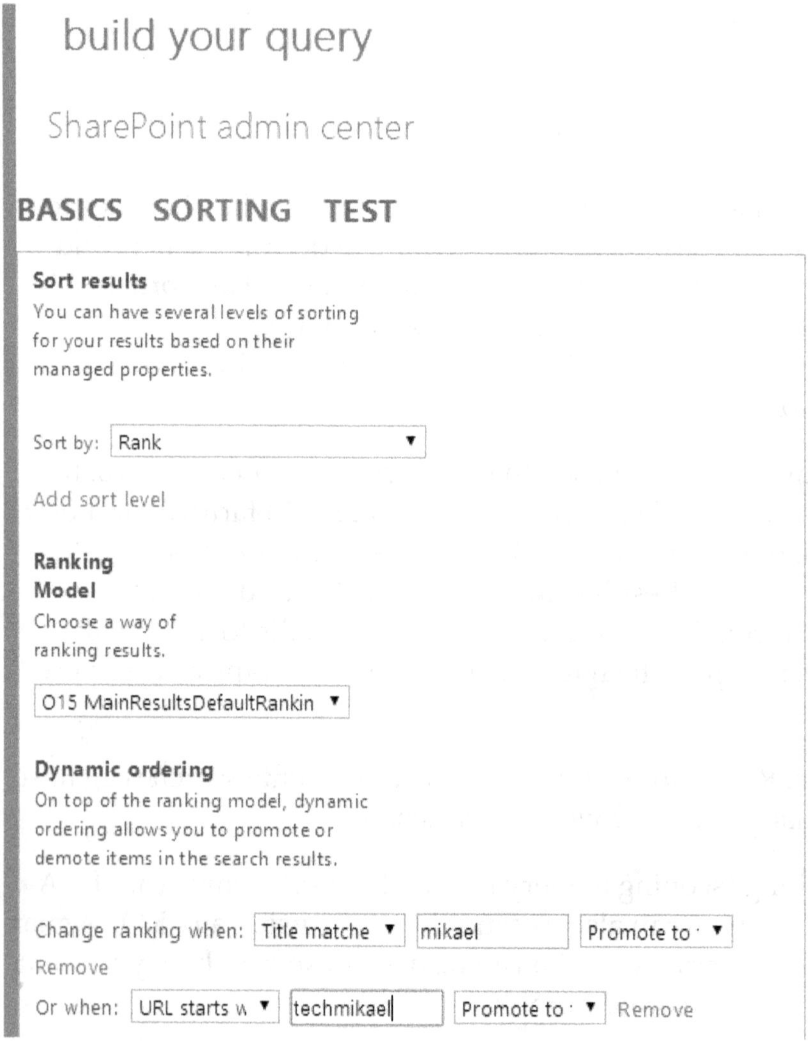

build your query

SharePoint admin center

BASICS SORTING TEST

Sort results

You can have several levels of sorting for your results based on their managed properties.

Sort by: Rank

Add sort level

Ranking Model

Choose a way of ranking results.

O15 MainResultsDefaultRankin

Dynamic ordering

On top of the ranking model, dynamic ordering allows you to promote or demote items in the search results.

Change ranking when: Title matche mikael Promote to

Remove

Or when: URL starts w techmikael Promote to Remove

In addition to all of the above, a result source can be used to specify a different set of credentials to use when querying that particular result source (mostly used for OpenSearch as it's limited to basic authentication).

If you start off with a the default enterprise search center in SharePoint, then all the tabs/result pages are pre-configured to use different result sources.

Everything People Conversations Videos

Tab Name	Result Source
Everything	Local SharePoint Results
People	Local People Results
Conversations	Conversations
Videos	Local Video Results

The above four result sources are defined at the Search Service Application (SSA) or tenant level in SharePoint Online, and they are all limiting the results coming from the SharePoint index to display a subset.

A result source may reside or be scoped to three different levels. The SSA, per site collection or per site (per tenant being the fourth). Where you decide to create your result source depends largely on the re-use scenarios for the result source. A result source created at a higher level, is always accessible at a lower level. This means a result source created at the SSA level is available on any site, but a result sources created at one particular site, is only available on that one site.

As an example a result source which limit the results to documents you have authored on the current site you are viewing is suitable as an SSA result source, as it can use a query variable to pick up the current site, and then be re-used all at any site collection or site in your SharePoint farm/tenant.

SharePoint already provides such a result source named *Items related to current user*, which also includes list items in addition to documents.

{?path:{Scope}} {?owstaxIdMetadataAllTagsInfo:{Tag}} {?ContentTypeId:{ContentTypeId}} People:{User} (IsDocument:"True" OR contentclass:"STS_ListItem")

You should always use Result Sources

The two web parts you will be using the most with result sources are the *Content Search Web Part* and the *Search Result Web Part*. Both of these allow you to specify a query transformation directly, so unless you are targeting an OpenSearch source, you probably have done this already. You edit the page, edit the web part, kick off the Query Builder, make your adjustments, click OK, save the web part changes, save the page, check it in, and maybe even publish and approve a new version.

Then you figure out you need to make a change, edit the page, edit the web part, kick off the Query Builder, make your adjustments once more, click OK, save the web part changes, save the page, check it in... phew! A few more iterations of this and you see where I'm heading.

If you instead create a result source, and hook your web part up to that source, you only need to save the web part and the page **once**! All further changes are achieved at the result source instead. Edit result source, kick off Query Builder, click OK, click Save. Wait 5-10 seconds, refresh your page and you can see your changes live and clear!

Tip: If you create web templates which you use search to surface up information, then creating a result source on the site collection level which all sub-sites re-use is an excellent use case of site collection scoped result sources.

A use case for a site scoped result source could be a user creating a new page and wanting to administer what is displayed on that page only without having to do the page edit dance (provided the user has site administrative rights).

All the query examples from the previous chapters in this book are suitable to be used as Result Sources, and remember to **name your result sources with meaningful names**! Makes administration later that much easier.

Result Sources and Query Rules

Result sources also closely relate to query rules, where a particular rule will change a query executed against a specific result source. You can, as with the web parts, change the query in the query rule itself, but hooking them up with well named result sources might work just as well and allows you to separate rule logic from what is displayed. The usage of query rules will be covered in Chapters 5-8.

Off topic – Display Templates

This is a bit outside the scope of this book, but important to mention. If you create custom display templates you often hook them up to custom Result Types. If you don't, you really should.

For example, you might create a display template which renders blog posts a certain way. And you might also have a result source *Blog Posts* which limits results to blog posts only. In the Result Type, you may then set a matching condition to use this result type/display template for items coming from that particular result source.

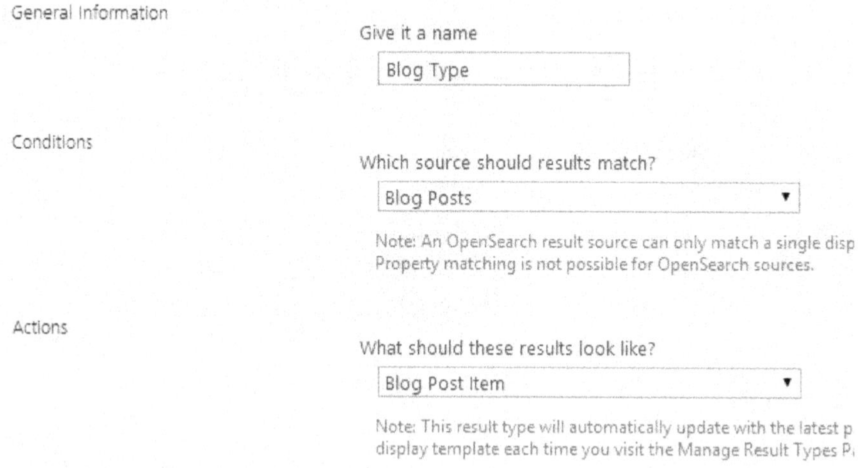

If you are displaying results of different types in your results and are using custom managed properties in your Display Templates, maintaining a 1:1 relationship between your Result Types and Display Templates is the only sure way which will make sure all properties are working for all display usages of a result type. It be in the main results or in a result block using the Search Result Web Part.

Summary

At the high level a result source is used to scope results to a particular sub-set. Using them wisely with search web parts will greatly cut down on the edit time spent testing out new queries, as changing a result source is much quicker than changing the query of a web part. Chapter 10 shows how you can use result sources in a smart way to orchestrate a search driven page.

References

Understanding result sources for search in SharePoint Server 2013
http://technet.microsoft.com/en-us/library/dn186229(v=office.15).aspx

Chapter 5

Query Rules Basics

I want to start out by saying: Query Rules Rule!! And in a big way!

If you are coming from SharePoint 2010 and used the search keywords feature for synonyms and best bets, then Query Rules is the brand new revved up engine which took its place. Think an old Toyota with a 1.4l engine, being replaced by a Tesla Model S (or the movie *The Expendables* without steroids).

So what is a query rule exactly? When a search query is being executed, one or more query rules can, based on specified conditions, intercept the query and take actions on it.

The available actions are:

1. Add promoted results (Best Bets in 2010)
2. Add one or more result blocks, which are additional groups of results or side results to the original result
3. Re-write the query
4. Change the sorting or ranking of the results

General Information

Rule name

Query Rules!

Fires only on source Local SharePoint Results.

▷ Context

Query Conditions

Define when a user's search box query makes this rule fire. You can specify multiple conditions of different types, or remove all conditions to fire for any query text. Every query condition becomes false if the query is not a simple keyword query, such as if it has quotes, property filters, parentheses, or special operators.

Query Matches Keyword Exactly ▼

Query exactly matches one of these phrases (semi-colon separated)

Remove Condition

Add Alternate Condition

Actions

When your rule fires, it can enhance search results in three ways. It can add promoted results above the ranked results. It can also add blocks of additional results. Like normal results, these blocks can be promoted to always appear above ranked results or ranked so they only appear if highly relevant. Finally, the rule can change ranked results, such as tuning their ordering.

Promoted Results

Add Promoted Result ①

Result Blocks

Add Result Block ②

Change ranked results by changing the query ③ ④

Promoted Results

A promoted result is an authored result which is added to the top of the search results. For example if a user searches for *search blog*, you can at the top of the results show a link or banner pointing to this blog.

For the promoted result you add a title, the URL and a description. You may also check to show it as a banner, and it will then load the URL content in an iframe instead.

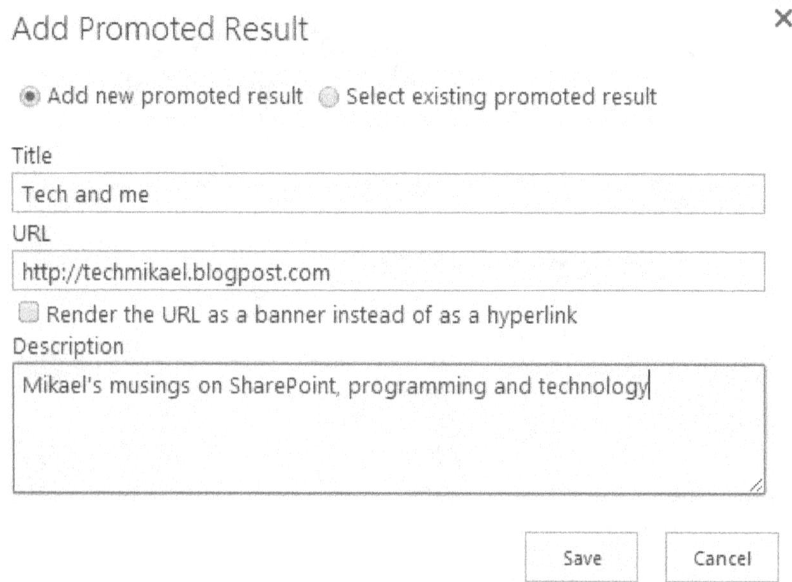

Promoted results will be displayed above the regular results.

Search

search blog 

Results found in
Gruppeområde for mAdcOW deZign

Preference for results in
English

✓ Tech and me
Mikael's musings on SharePoint, programming and technology
techmikael.blogspot.com/

tech&me
Welcome to my **blog** ... by Mikael Svenson on 8/20/2013 11:40 PM ... This is where I'll be sharing my thoughts on topics that matter ... **Search** help and community Looking for recommendations ...
techmikael.sharepoint.com/techandme

tech&me - Posts
Published Category # Comments Edit Rating (0-5 ... Welcome to my **blog**! Mikael Svenson 8/20/2013 11:40 PM 0 ... **Search** help and community Looking for recommendations ...
techmikael.sharepoint.com/techandme/Lists/Posts/AllPosts.aspx

The use cases are many and it's possible to override the way it displays with either a custom display template or CSS overrides. If you start adding lots and lots of promoted results and have enterprise licenses, you might want to switch tactics and use a custom list for promoted results instead. It requires a bit more initial work up-front, but will make it easier to maintain. See the post Better Best Bets with Lists (*http://techmikael.blogspot.com/2014/07/better-best-bets-with-lists.html*) for a detailed description on how this could be solved.

Result Blocks

Out of the box SharePoint comes with a whole list of pre-defined query rules which will add result blocks based on trigger words. One of them will trigger on the term *blog* anywhere in the query, and list items based on the blog web template in SharePoint.

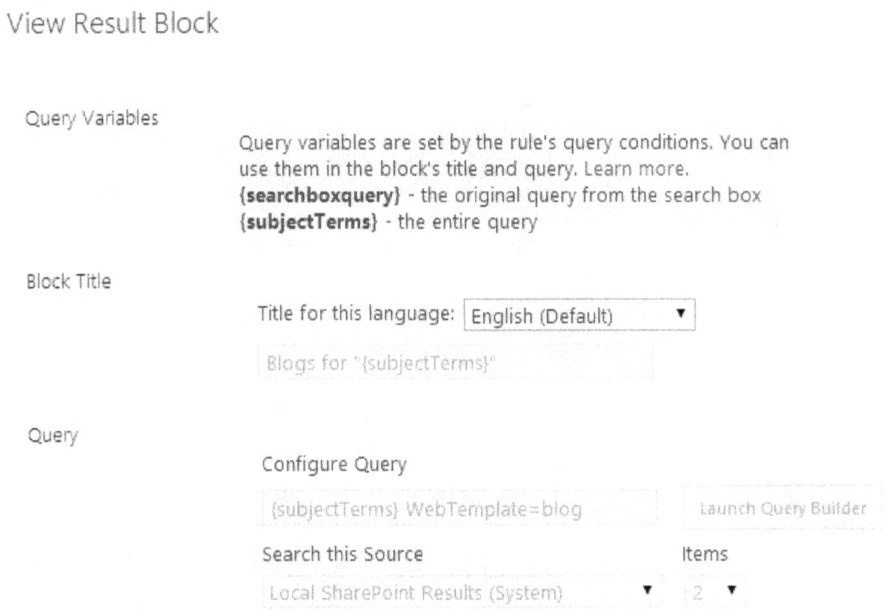

View Result Block

Query Variables

Query variables are set by the rule's query conditions. You can use them in the block's title and query. Learn more.
{searchboxquery} - the original query from the search box
{subjectTerms} - the entire query

Block Title

Title for this language: English (Default)

Blogs for "{subjectTerms}"

Query

Configure Query

{subjectTerms} WebTemplate=blog

Launch Query Builder

Search this Source

Local SharePoint Results (System)

Items

2

Performing the search *search blog* as in the previous example, you now get a block showing blog content hits from SharePoint at the top. Below the block, you get regular results. Something to note about result blocks is that they don't have to appear at the top. This particular one will actually move down in the results if no one ever clicks on the items inside the block region. And eventually it will move out of page 1 etc. This means that the users decide if the block is important or not, not the person creating the rule (unless it's chosen to always appear at the top).

Note: Result blocks are only available for users with enterprise licenses (e-CAL) assigned.

Search

search blog 

Results found in
Gruppeområde for mAdcOW deZign ▾

Preference for results in
English ▾

✓ Tech and me
Mikael's musings on SharePoint, programming and technology
techmikael.blogspot.com/

Blogger for search

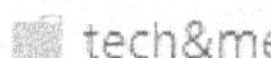 tech&me
Welcome to my **blog** ... by Mikael Svenson on 8/20/2013 11:40 PM ... This is where I'll be sharing my thoughts on topics that matter ... **Search** help and community Looking for recommendations ...
techmikael.sharepoint.com/techandme

tech&me - Posts
Published Category # Comments Edit Rating (0-5 ... Welcome to my **blog**! Mikael Svenson 8/20/2013 11:40 PM 0 ... **Search** help and community Looking for recommendations ...
techmikael.sharepoint.com/techandme/Lists/Posts/AllPosts.aspx

Re-write the query

In the above example with the blog result block, there is actually a query rewrite going on: *{subjectTerms} WebTemplate=blog*. It uses the original query and adds a property query to limit results from *WebTemplate* equals *blog*. That's all there is to it, and you have the full list of query variables at your disposal as well. If you've been reading the previous chapters in this book, it should start to come together, and you are getting close to being able to **turn business rules into query rules** - which coincidentally happens to be my #1 favorite search slogan.

It is also possible to use query rules for synonym expansion where you trigger on a term, and then add one or more terms. For example if someone searches for *Puzzlepart* you may want to rewrite the query as *Puzzlepart OR pzl OR puzlepart OR puzzelpart* to include any abbreviations or spelling mistakes.

Change sorting or ranking

In addition to re-writing the search queries, a query rule can also change the sorting or ranking of the results. Say you want your blog posts to appear with the newest first, then sort on *LastModifiedTime* in descending order.

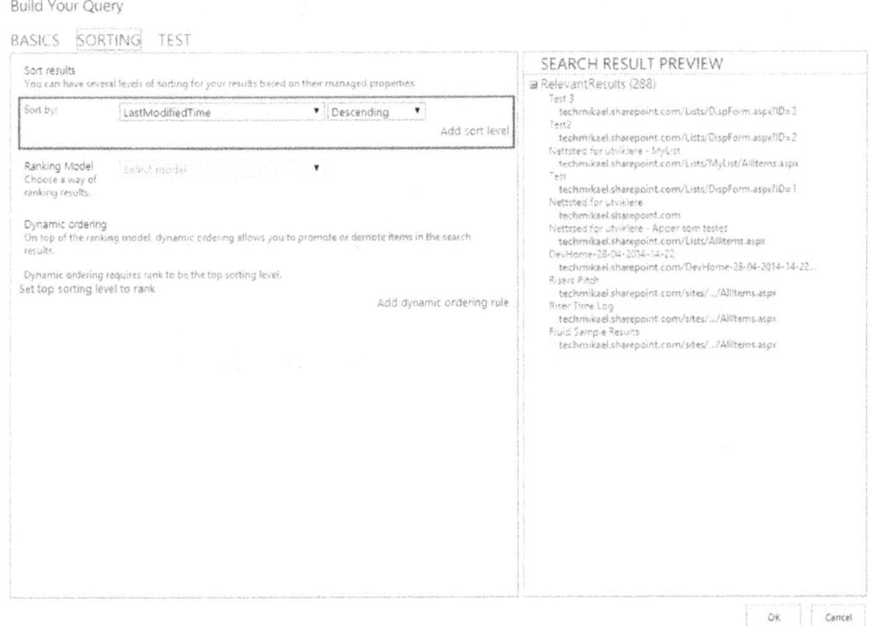

As with result sources, query rules can be created at the Search Service Application (tenant) level, site collection level and site level. Where you create them depends on how much you want to re-use their logic. By default there are a lot of rules coming out the box, attached to the out of the box result sources. I recommend heading over to a query rule settings page near you to take a look at the existing rules and familiarize yourself with them.

It is also possible to set a start and end date for a rule, which means you can have the promoted result about the upcoming summer party only appear up until the party is over.

Local SharePoint Results have the most rules included by far, and you might find that the rules trigger on your custom search sites without you wanting them to. The quickest solution to this is to create your own result source, equal to that one of Local SharePoint Results, and use that source as your basis. Then you can add one and one rule as you see the need.

Summary - Query Rules Rule!

Hopefully after reading this chapter you should have a brief overview of what query rules are, and what they can do for you. Chapter 6 will cover more in-depth how to use the different options of query rules.

References

Understanding query rules
https://support.office.com/en-us/article/Understanding-query-rules-8ca2588d-9dc7-45aa-90a4-428d4d695d07?ui=en-US&rs=en-US&ad=US

Manage query rules (SharePoint Online)
https://support.office.com/en-us/article/Manage-query-rules-53556bb4-3625-490b-aa89-1223e3d4ce3f?ui=en-US&rs=en-US&ad=US

Manage query rules in SharePoint Server 2013
http://technet.microsoft.com/en-us/library/jj871676(v=office.15).aspx

Better Best Bets with Lists
http://techmikael.blogspot.se/2014/07/better-best-bets-with-lists.html

Chapter 6

Rewriting using Query Rules

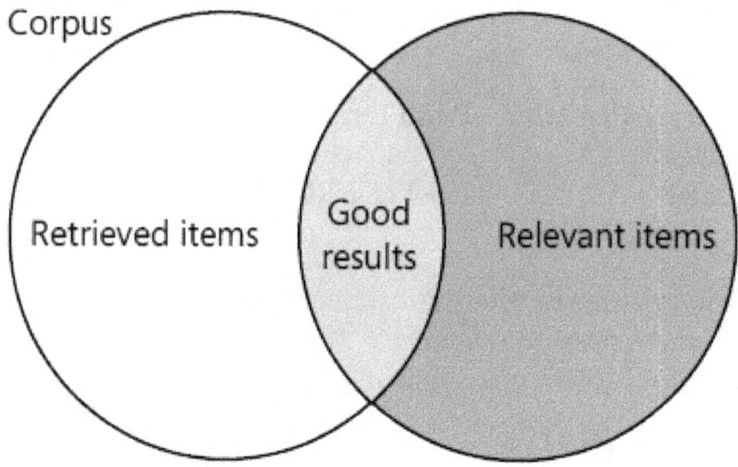

Two key concepts in search are recall and precision. *Recall* refers to the number of results a search engine returns for a specific query, and *precision* refers to how precisely the results match the search user's intent. You must make a compromise between recall and precision. If recall is too large, you essentially flood the result set with noise, and precision suffers. On the other hand, when recall is too small, you run the risk of missing useful results, so the item(s) the user is looking for may not appear in the result set; again, precision suffers.

And this is where Query Rules play a part in SharePoint. By looking at the queries coming in, you have the option to change them to better match your content, and thus improve on recall and precision.

By default, recall in SharePoint search is expanded using a multitude of linguistic features to make sure variants of the terms entered are included. For example a search for *test* would also include *test*, and vice versa.

Example 1 – improve recall

Say in your domain, the term *test,* also means *exam* and *certification.* Then you could use a query rule to expand on this (In SharePoint on-premises this could also be achieved using a thesaurus using PowerShell). The image below will do a two way synonym expansion, where it will match on either *test, exam* or *certification,* and expand with the same terms.

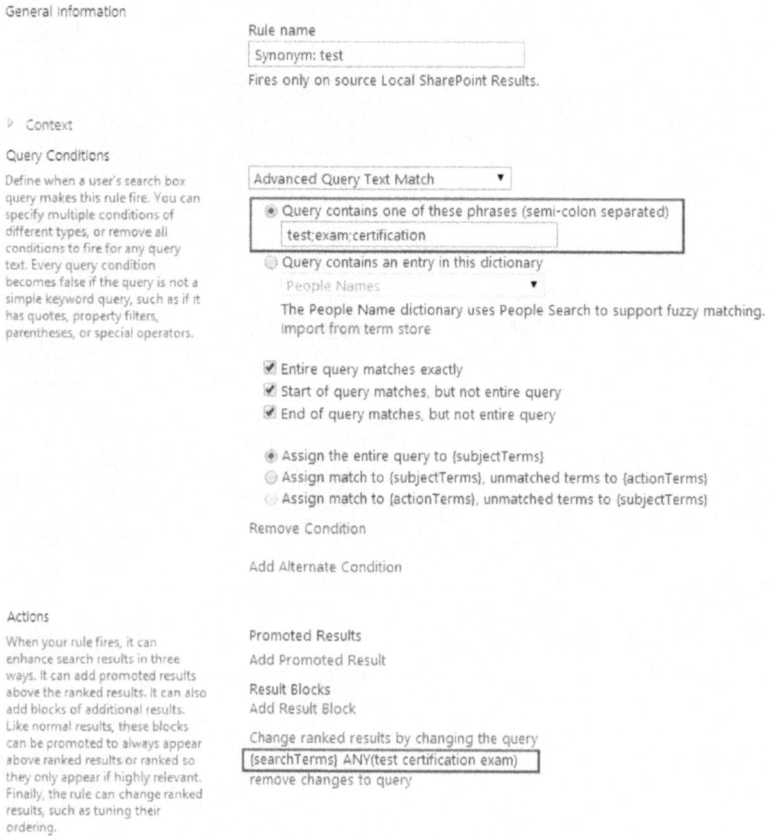

General Information

Rule name

Synonym: test

Fires only on source Local SharePoint Results.

Context

Query Conditions

Define when a user's search box query makes this rule fire. You can specify multiple conditions of different types, or remove all conditions to fire for any query text. Every query condition becomes false if the query is not a simple keyword query, such as if it has quotes, property filters, parentheses, or special operators.

Advanced Query Text Match

Query contains one of these phrases (semi-colon separated)

test;exam;certification

Query contains an entry in this dictionary

People Names

The People Name dictionary uses People Search to support fuzzy matching.

Import from term store

Entire query matches exactly

Start of query matches, but not entire query

End of query matches, but not entire query

Assign the entire query to {subjectTerms}

Assign match to {subjectTerms}, unmatched terms to {actionTerms}

Assign match to {actionTerms}, unmatched terms to {subjectTerms}

Remove Condition

Add Alternate Condition

Actions

When your rule fires, it can enhance search results in three ways. It can add promoted results above the ranked results. It can also add blocks of additional results. Like normal results, these blocks can be promoted to always appear above ranked results or ranked so they only appear if highly relevant. Finally, the rule can change ranked results, such as tuning their ordering.

Promoted Results

Add Promoted Result

Result Blocks

Add Result Block

Change ranked results by changing the query

{searchTerms} ANY(test certification exam)

remove changes to query

In the above example I chose to use the *Advanced Query Text Match* condition, where I checked entire query, start and end matching. This means that the term test has to either be at the start or end of the query, or be by itself. In the list below the first three will match, while the last will not.

- sharepoint test
- test sharepoint
- test
- lets test sharepoint

If you are on-premises you have the option of writing regular expressions, and using regular expressions you can do about as advanced matches as you want.

Example 2 – improve precision

Another rewriting example can be to turn natural language into valid KQL syntax. Let's say a user types in: *sales report last month,* then you could turn that into the following rule.

General Information

Rule name

Limit: last month

Fires only on source Local SharePoint Results.

Context

Query Conditions

Define when a user's search box query makes this rule fire. You can specify multiple conditions of different types, or remove all conditions to fire for any query text. Every query condition becomes false if the query is not a simple keyword query, such as if it has quotes, property filters, parentheses, or special operators.

Advanced Query Text Match

- (•) Query contains one of these phrases (semi-colon separated)
  last month
- ( ) Query contains an entry in this dictionary
  People Names
  The People Name dictionary uses People Search to support fuzzy matching.
  Import from term store

- [ ] Entire query matches exactly
- [ ] Start of query matches, but not entire query
- [x] End of query matches, but not entire query

- ( ) Assign the entire query to {subjectTerms}
- ( ) Assign match to {subjectTerms}, unmatched terms to {actionTerms}
- (•) Assign match to {actionTerms}, unmatched terms to {subjectTerms}

Remove Condition

Add Alternate Condition

Actions

When your rule fires, it can enhance search results in three ways. It can add promoted results above the ranked results. It can also add blocks of additional results. Like normal results, these blocks can be promoted to always appear above ranked results or ranked so they only appear if highly relevant. Finally, the rule can change ranked results, such as tuning their ordering.

Promoted Results

Add Promoted Result

Result Blocks

Add Result Block

Change ranked results by changing the query

{subjectTerms} write:"last month"

remove changes to query

First decide to trigger on *last month* at the end of the query. Then check that the trigger term is assigned to the *{actionTerms}* variable and the rest of the query, *sales report,* to *{subjectTerms}*. In the query rewrite use *{subjectTerms}* and append a filter on the write property using one of the special date filters mentioned in Chapter 1, to limit results to those of last month only. The ending query would look like: *sales report write:"last month"*.

Summary

In order to provide better end-results for your users you can start to examine your search logs for common queries. Then apply your domain knowledge to those queries and add query rules which change those queries into what the user actually meant. This is hard for a computer to do, but as someone who knows the content you can apply your own smartness to help out your users.

References

Linguistic search features in SharePoint Server 2013
http://technet.microsoft.com/en-us/library/jj219499(v=office.15).aspx

Create and deploy a thesaurus in SharePoint Server 2013
http://technet.microsoft.com/en-us/library/jj219579(v=office.15).aspx

Chapter 7

Sorting results using Query Rules

Chapter 6 discussed the concepts of RECALL and PRECISION which has to do with bringing back relevant items for a search query. When you have your golden set of items, the next step is to sort them in the best order possible to ensure the most relevant items are in your top hits or first page of results.

Tip: Increase the default number of items to display to 25 or 50. Ten items is not a lot and people are getting more and more used to scrolling these days (if you want to go above 50, JavaScript sorcery is needed as the web parts are hard coded to max 50).

There are four ways to sort a result in SharePoint:

- Sort the results based on a ranking profile
  - *You may also influence ranking by using the XRANK keyword (dynamic ordering)*
- Sort the results based on a managed property ascending or descending
- Sort the results based on a **sorting formula**
- Sort the results randomly
  - *This is accommodated using a special sorting formula*

Using query rules the first two options listed above are available (rank and managed property) using the Query Builder interface in SharePoint. If you want to sort by formula in a query rule you will have to export the search configuration, edit the XML manually and import it back in. The property field will then show empty in the query builder as seen below.

```
<d8p1:KeyValueOfstringanyType>
    <d8p1:Key>SortList</d8p1:Key>
    <d8p1:Value i:type="d4p1:SortCollection">
        <d4p1:m_elements>
            <d4p1:Sort>
               <d4p1:direction>Ascending</d4p1:direction>
               <d4p1:strProperty>[random:seed=5432]</d4p1:strProperty>
            </d4p1:Sort>
        </d4p1:m_elements>
    </d8p1:Value>
</d8p1:KeyValueOfstringanyType>
```

Build Your Query

BASICS SORTING TEST

Sort results

You can have several levels of sorting for your results based on their managed properties.

Sort by: Ascending

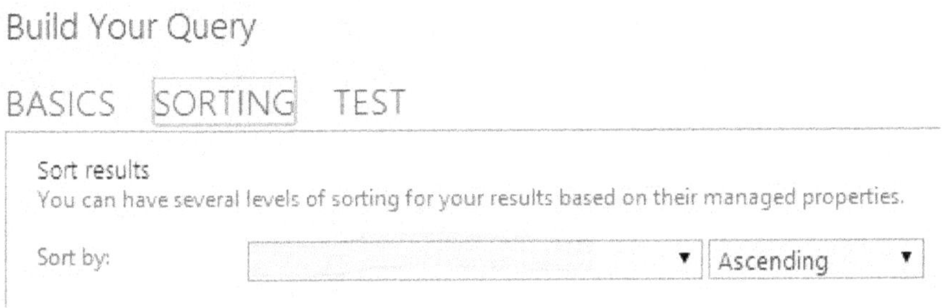

You can have a total of five sorting levels defined for a query rule. If you are using rank as a sorting level, it has to be the first level, and you can only specify one ranking level.

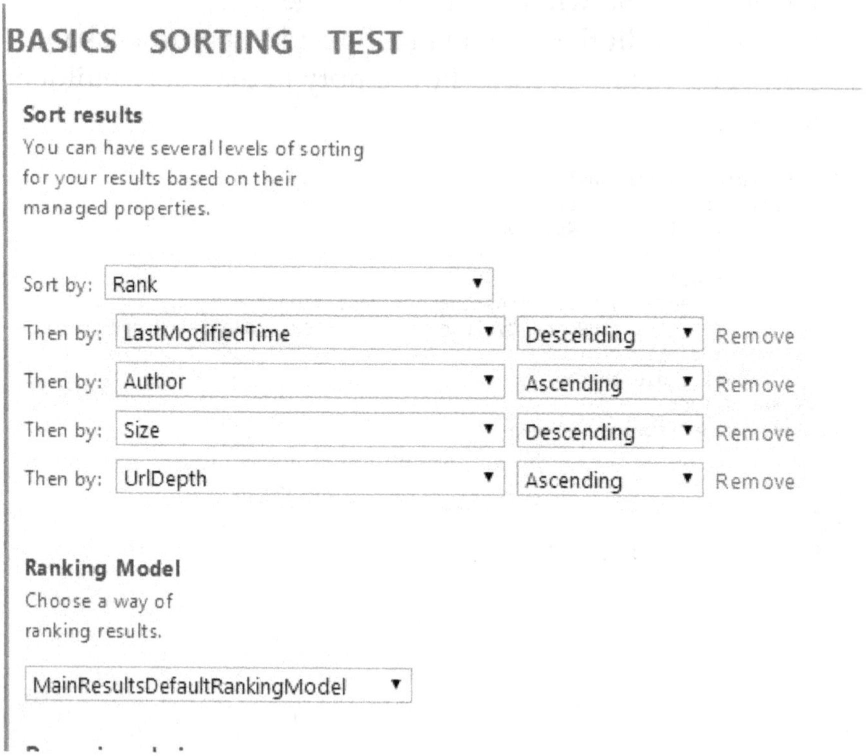

BASICS SORTING TEST

Sort results

You can have several levels of sorting for your results based on their managed properties.

Sort by:	Rank		
Then by:	LastModifiedTime	Descending	Remove
Then by:	Author	Ascending	Remove
Then by:	Size	Descending	Remove
Then by:	UrlDepth	Ascending	Remove

Ranking Model

Choose a way of ranking results.

MainResultsDefaultRankingModel

More Information: The schema definition for query rule sorting as specified in 3.1.4.7.4.4 SortDirection at MSDN states that in order to use a formula for sorting, you should specify FQLFormula as the SortDirection property. While this work, it won't let you specify a direction of the sorting. If you want to specify which direction your sorting should, keep Ascending/Descending as the SortDirection, and write your formula in brackets [] as per Sort search results by a formula expression, and not with regular FQL as stated in the specification. This is equal to the code shown earlier in this chapter where the random formula was used.

There can only be one (rule to sort them all)

One very important thing to note if you are changing the sort order using Query Rules is that only **ONE** rule can apply sorting to your results. If you have more than one rule triggering and changing the sort order, then neither will be applied.

If you have more than one rule which sets sort logic, where both can in theory trigger, then you need to add the query rules to a group, put them in the right order, and set STOP for each rule. This implies that sorting rules should be ordered to the bottom of all your rules.

Sorting by rank

The default sorting in SharePoint is to use the default rank profile. It is possible to create custom rank profiles, but that's a book by itself.

The dynamic part however is very much within grasp by using XRANK. The easiest route to using XRANK for promoting or demoting items is to add a dynamic ordering rule using the query builder. The example below promotes items which contain the name *Mikael*.

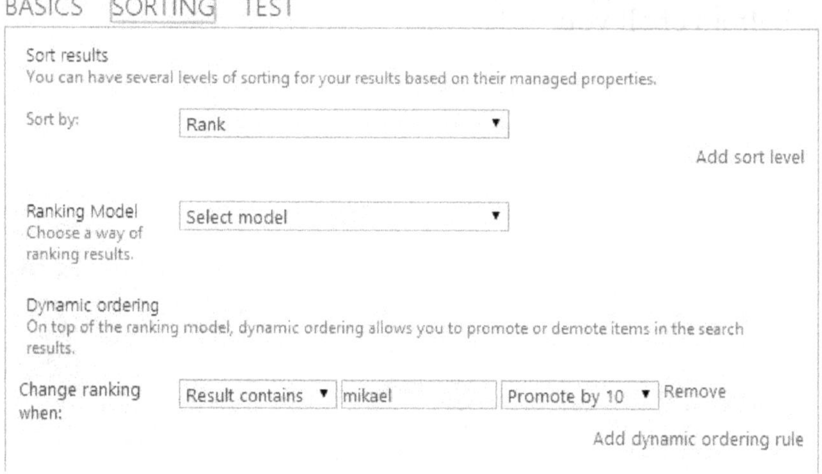

Clicking the *TEST* tab will reveal the final query for this setting.

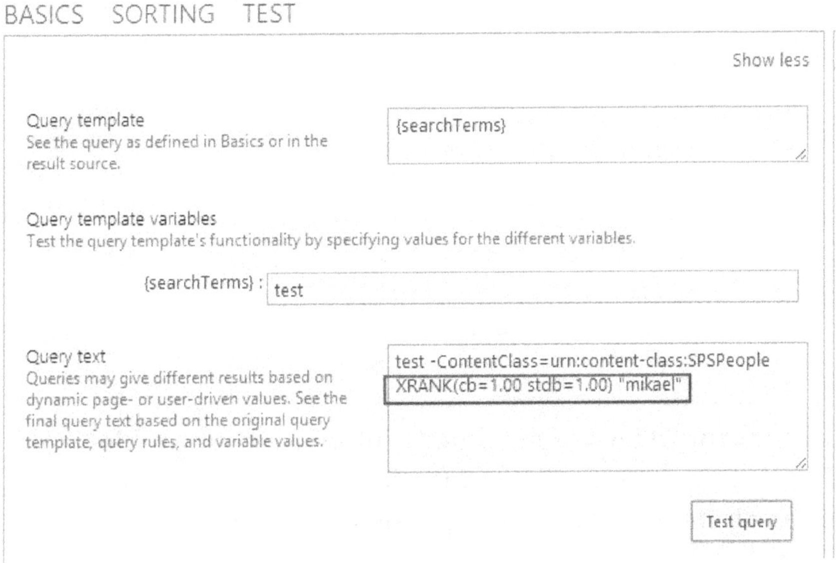

BASICS SORTING TEST

Show less

Query template
See the query as defined in Basics or in the result source.

{searchTerms}

Query template variables
Test the query template's functionality by specifying values for the different variables.

{searchTerms} : test

Query text
Queries may give different results based on dynamic page- or user-driven values. See the final query text based on the original query template, query rules, and variable values.

test -ContentClass=urn:content-class:SPSPeople XRANK(cb=1.00 stdb=1.00) "mikael"

Test query

The drawback of using the Sorting builder is that you cannot make variable ranking conditions (shown in example three, Chapter 3). If you want full control you can experiment by using the builder, then take the final query and paste it into the Query box yourself.

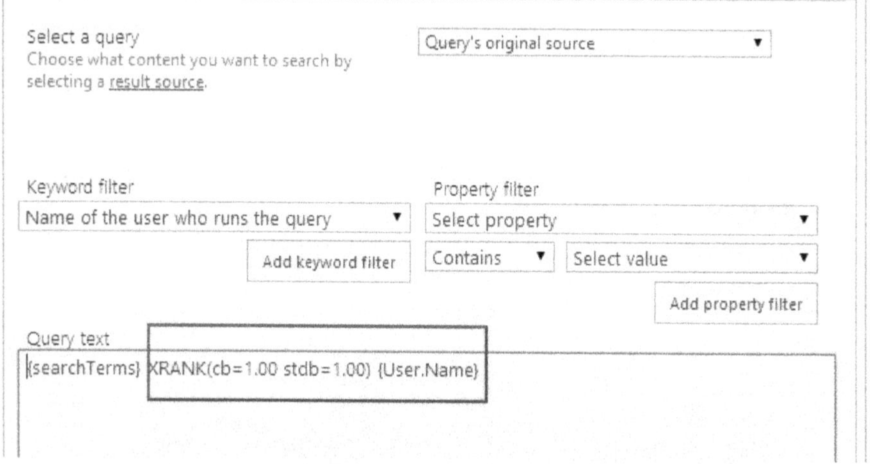

If you want last modified date to influence your ranking, take a look at my blog post about freshness boost, or add it as part of a custom rank model (not possible in SharePoint Online).

Sorting by managed property

Any managed property marked as *Sortable* can be used to sort your results. Typically news articles should be sorted by last modified time in descending order, to show the newest articles first.

When searching for people in a directory you might want to first sort on last name, then on first name, as opposed to social distance.

Sorting by formula

If you have a product catalog with both the price you are paying and the price you are selling it for in separate managed properties, you could sort items by highest margin.

[outprice-inprice]:descending

Formula sorting can be applied to managed properties of type Integer, Decimal and Datetime. The properties also have to be marked as sortable.

Summary

How you order search results is an important part of presenting your search results. By transforming business rules to query rules, you can change how items are ordered to create better search experiences for your end users. It's also possible to set sorting both at result sources and web parts directly, but using rules you can trigger sorting based on different criteria.

References

Sorting search results in SharePoint 2013
http://msdn.microsoft.com/en-us/library/office/jj938031(v=office.15).aspx

SortDirection specification
http://msdn.microsoft.com/en-us/library/ff389400(v=office.12).aspx

Adding freshness boost in SharePoint Online
http://techmikael.blogspot.com/2013/10/adding-freshness-boost-to-sharepoint.html

Chapter 8

Intent based triggering of Query Rules

This fourth chapter on query rules will focus on capturing the intent of the user. What is the person searching really looking for? If you look at a random query log you can, more often than not, easily pick out queries which you could call *"Q and A queries"*. By *"Q and A query"* I mean a query which is meant to bring back an answer which you can take action on right away.

Examples

Question (query)	**Answer (result)**
sales report oslo	List sales reports for oslo, with newest on top
pain killers	Where can I locate pain killers in the office
company presentation	The most up to date company PowerPoint presentation
developer blog posts	Blog posts about development
mikael svenson	Information about me :-)

The common denominator for all of the above queries is that the terms themselves can be used to rewrite the query to provide better results for the end-user. If you don't turn business rules into query rules, the top 10 results on your page will likely not have the answer to all of these questions.

Chapter 6 and 7 already touched on some ways to re-write queries, so let's use some of the previously acquired knowledge to solve the five questions above.

Query: sales report oslo

For this one create a rule which trigger on *sales report* and limits the results to only sales reports. Then order the results with the last modified ones on top, as the user is more likely to want fresher content.

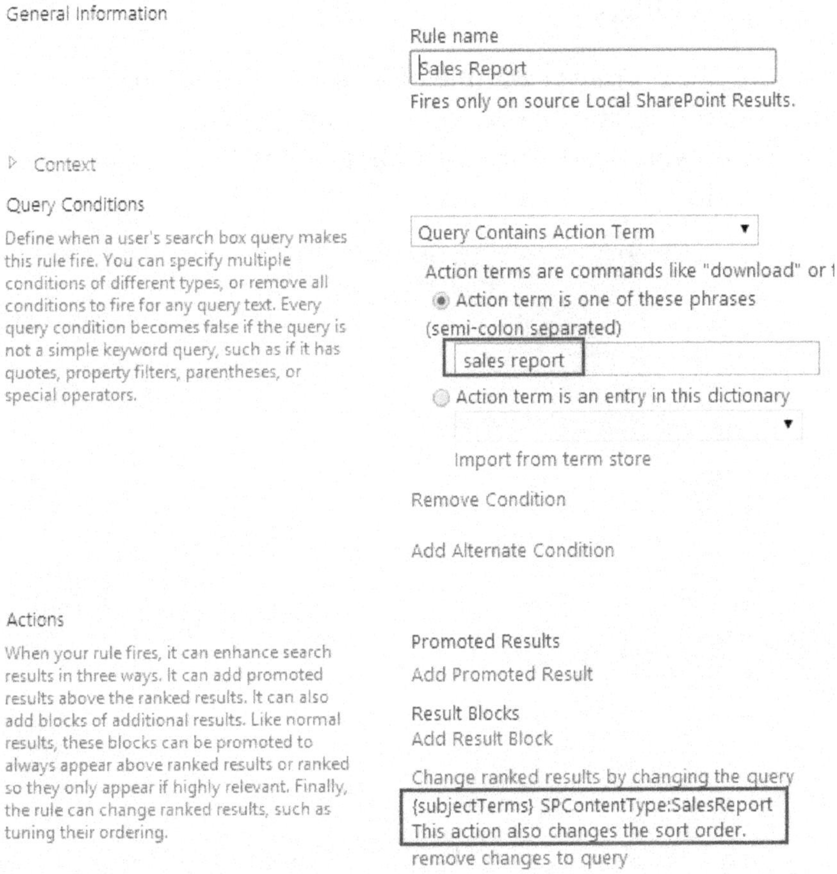

General Information

Rule name

Sales Report

Fires only on source Local SharePoint Results.

Context

Query Conditions

Define when a user's search box query makes this rule fire. You can specify multiple conditions of different types, or remove all conditions to fire for any query text. Every query condition becomes false if the query is not a simple keyword query, such as if it has quotes, property filters, parentheses, or special operators.

Query Contains Action Term

Action terms are commands like "download" or t

Action term is one of these phrases (semi-colon separated)

sales report

Action term is an entry in this dictionary

Import from term store

Remove Condition

Add Alternate Condition

Actions

When your rule fires, it can enhance search results in three ways. It can add promoted results above the ranked results. It can also add blocks of additional results. Like normal results, these blocks can be promoted to always appear above ranked results or ranked so they only appear if highly relevant. Finally, the rule can change ranked results, such as tuning their ordering.

Promoted Results

Add Promoted Result

Result Blocks

Add Result Block

Change ranked results by changing the query

{subjectTerms} SPContentType:SalesReport

This action also changes the sort order.

remove changes to query

Make a note of the *{subjectTerms}* variable which contains all query words except the trigger term. This means the final query would be:

oslo SPContentType:SalesReport

In the above query rule results are also ordered on *LastModifiedTime* in descending order.

Another possibility is to create a result source for sales reports, and display the results in a result block instead of changing the main results.

Query: pain killers

This query is a typical example of a best bet, or promoted result. There might be a document or a page with the information you need, but a best bet is much better suited for this scenario.

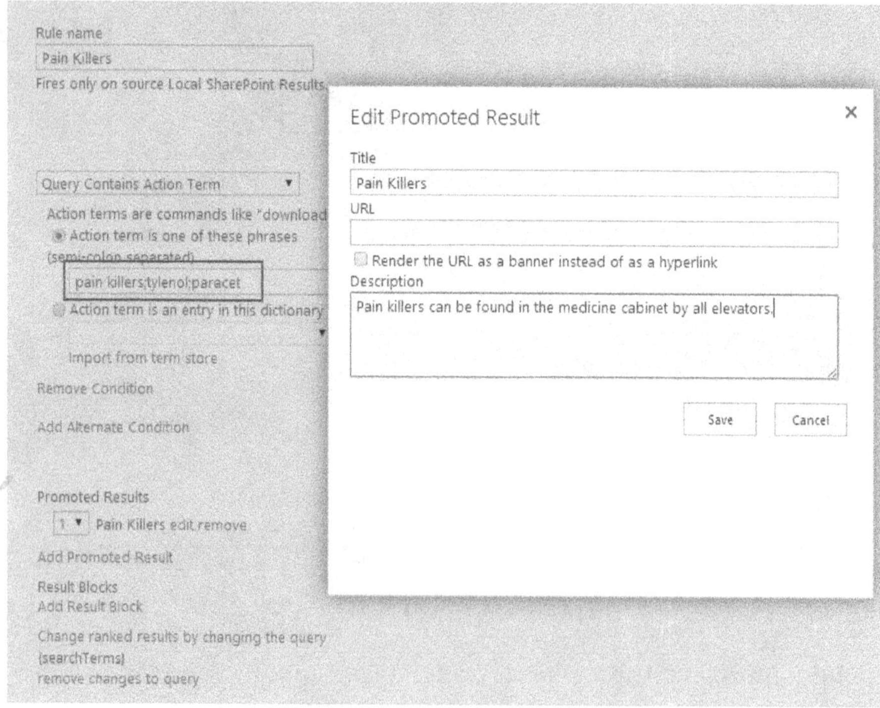

Query: company presentation

This is similar to *sales report*. One way is to trigger on both terms and list presentations by content type or location. Another is to trigger on only *presentation* limiting the results to PowerPoint files hoping the term *company* in itself will bring to the top what you want. Or, create a best bet. It all depends on your data and how you best can present the answer.

Query: developer blog posts

For this one let's trigger on *blog posts*. Next boost posts which have been tagged with developer, promoting them to the top of the result list.

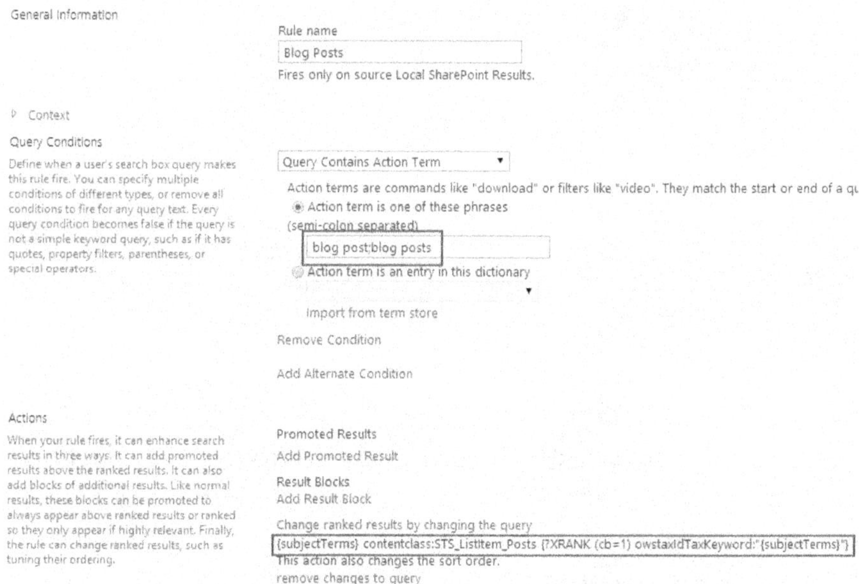

{subjectTerms} contentclass:STS_ListItem_Posts {?XRANK (cb=1) owstaxIdTaxKeyword:"{subjectTerms}"}

It's also possible to display a result block instead of changing the main results.

Query: mikael svenson

This one is easy by default as SharePoint provides a rule to match the names of people in your organization, and displays them in a result block.

General Information

Rule name

People Name in Sharepoint Search

Fires only on source Local SharePoint Results.

Context

Query Conditions

Define when a user's search box query makes this rule fire. You can specify multiple conditions of different types, or remove all conditions to fire for any query text. Every query condition becomes false if the query is not a simple keyword query, such as if it has quotes, property filters, parentheses, or special operators.

Query Matches Dictionary Exactly ▾

Query exactly matches an entry in this dictionary

People Names ▾

The People Name dictionary uses People Search to support fuzzy matching.

Actions

When your rule fires, it can enhance search results in three ways. It can add promoted results above the ranked results. It can also add blocks of additional results. Like normal results, these blocks can be promoted to always appear above ranked results or ranked so they only appear if highly relevant. Finally, the rule can change ranked results, such as tuning their ordering.

Promoted Results

Result Blocks

Promoted (shown above ranked results in this order)

People named "{subjectTerms}" view

Ranked (shown in ranked results when highly relevant)

Documents by "{subjectTerms}" view

You could however build this out to trigger on a list of only first names or only last names as well. To do this you have to get the list of names into a dictionary in the term store. If you are on-premises you could map first and last named fields from the User Profiles to custom term sets for this purpose. For SharePoint Online this is not possible and you would need to run code from the outside to create these dictionaries automatically.

Summary

Matching the intent of your users is a matter of understanding their queries, and change them to return what the user is actually looking for. Two good starting points are the search query logs and your own domain knowledge of your business!

Happy triggering!

References

Manage query rules
https://support.office.com/en-us/article/Manage-query-rules-53556bb4-3625-490b-aa89-1223e3d4ce3f?ui=en-US&rs=en-US&ad=US

Chapter 9

Context based triggering of Query Rules

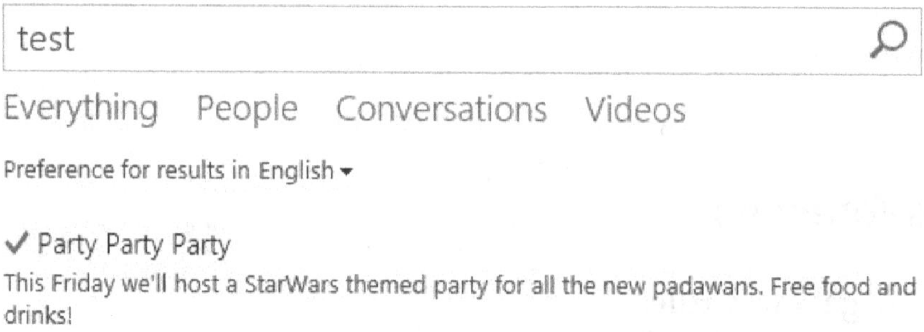

test

Everything People Conversations Videos

Preference for results in English

✓ Party Party Party

This Friday we'll host a StarWars themed party for all the new padawans. Free food and drinks!

Context capturing is one of the more interesting areas of search, but also one of the harder ones to get right. The overall concept is as follows:

For a specific group of users you change the search experience based on that group.

In the sample image above you see a promoted result for new employees who happen to like *StarWars*. It's a very simple concept, and a really powerful one. It's up to you to decide what your query rule should do with your result - promoted results, change sort order, change what is displayed etc...

In SharePoint 2013/Online the way to provide context aware experiences is to create a query rule which is triggered based on USER SEGMENTS.

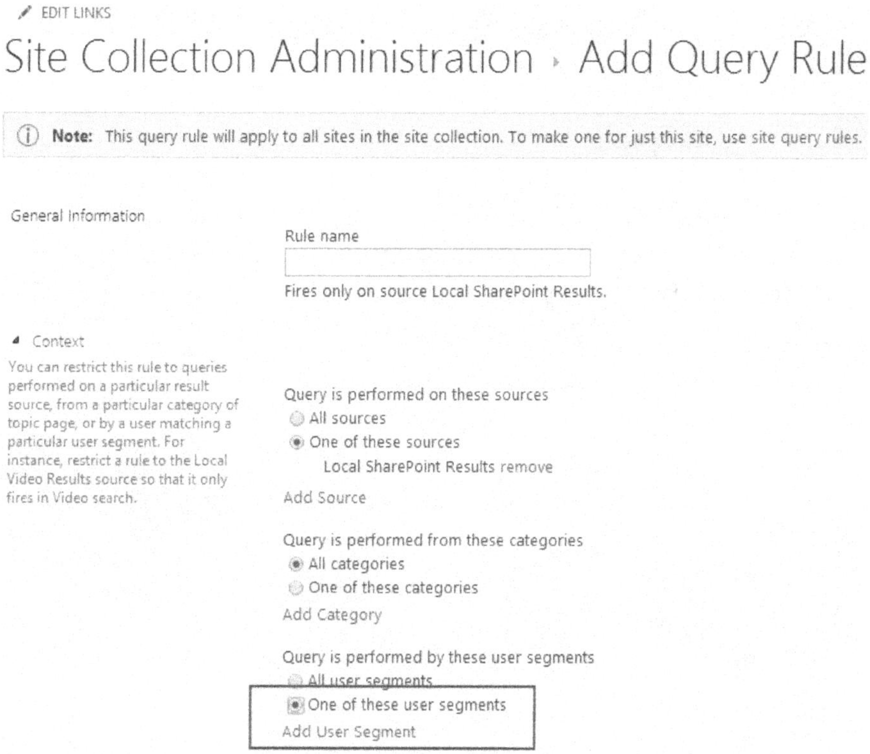

EDIT LINKS

Site Collection Administration › Add Query Rule

Note: This query rule will apply to all sites in the site collection. To make one for just this site, use site query rules.

General Information

Rule name

Fires only on source Local SharePoint Results.

Context

You can restrict this rule to queries performed on a particular result source, from a particular category of topic page, or by a user matching a particular user segment. For instance, restrict a rule to the Local Video Results source so that it only fires in Video search.

Query is performed on these sources
- All sources
- One of these sources
  Local SharePoint Results remove

Add Source

Query is performed from these categories
- All categories
- One of these categories

Add Category

Query is performed by these user segments
- All user segments
- One of these user segments

Add User Segment

Technically a user segment is a term in a term set, and it can be anything. It could be a term for the organization unit you work in, the kind of web browser you are using, your primary language, that you are newly employed, that you like to dress up as Luke Skywalker while searching on your intranet between 1 and 3 am in the morning. Anything! It's up to you to define the contexts you want to use to change the search results, and then tie the terms to query rules.

The hard part is how do you evaluate or create this context, so that it is used when a user searches in SharePoint?

Mantra: Turning business rules into query rules!

Create a term set named *Search Contexts,* and add two terms:

- New Guy
- StarWars Fetish

For the query rule add a new user segment named *New guy with SW likes,* which consists of these two terms. So, both of the terms have to be present in a search query for the rule to trigger.

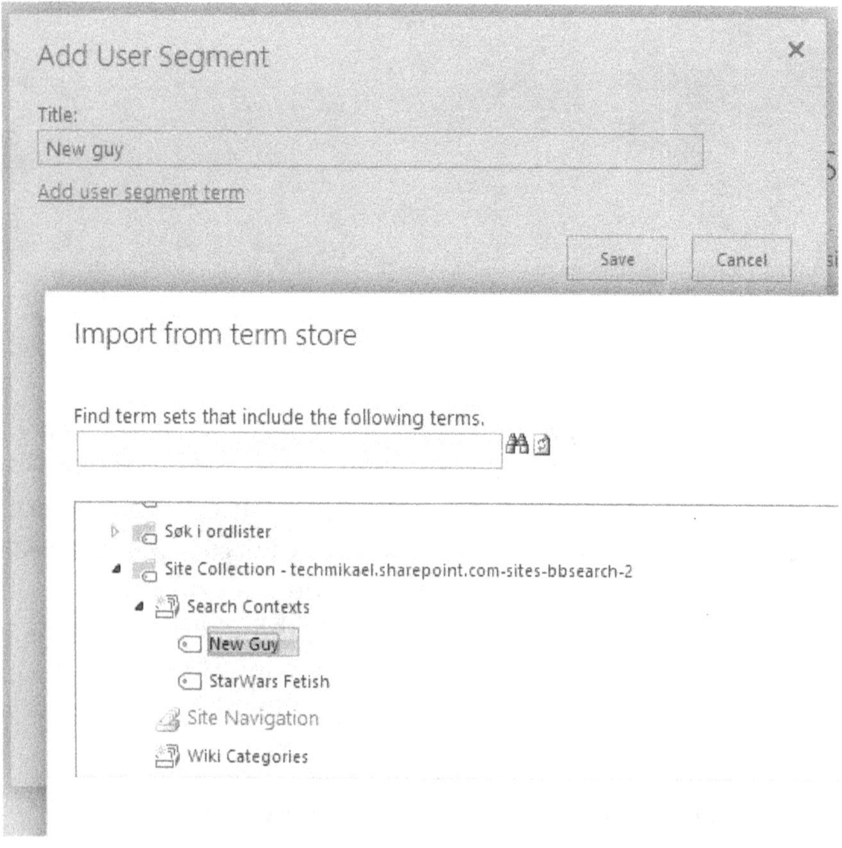

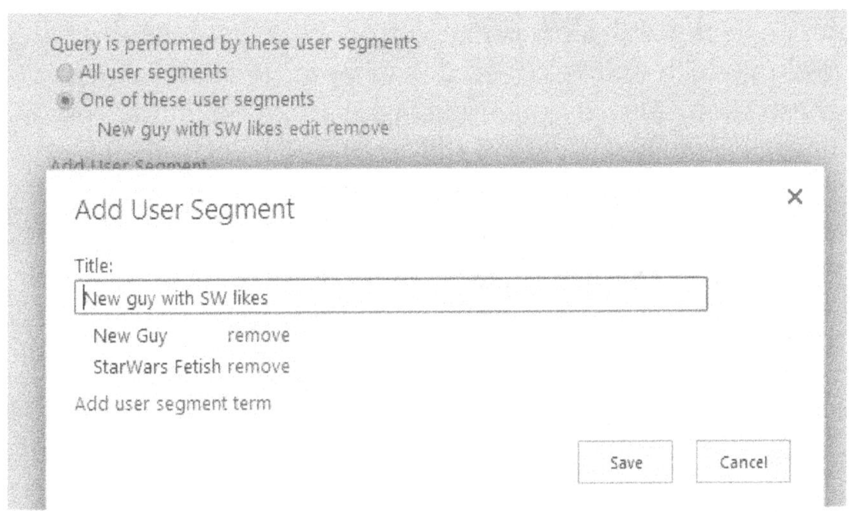

If you look at the reference links at the end of this episode you see that the samples tell you to create a new full trust web part, which will contain the business logic to evaluate your context, look up the term for it, and put the terms GUID in a variable named *UserSegmentTerms*. The query engine will then match the GUID's of from this variable against your query rules and trigger accordingly.

In the above example you could look at the employees start date to determine if he/she's a new guy or not. As for the interest in *StarWars* this could come from a user profile property of interests, or perhaps by examining his/her Facebook profile. When you have assembled the context, throw up a promoted results about the cool *StarWars* themed party for all the new hiring's on Friday.

And this is the difficult part. How do you assemble these contexts and make them not too dependent on external sources, as this will slow down your page. A somewhat hard question which will be covered in Chapter 10 about search orchestration. Also, if you are using SharePoint Online you cannot deploy these kinds of full trust web parts, and is left to bring out your JavaScript wand (see sample at *github.com/SPCSR* which I also used at SPC382 at the SharePoint Conference 2014).

For the promoted results example above you can use your browser developer tools to inject the GUID's for the context terms into the search context with the following JavaScript snippet.

```
// b34abf38-d746-4037-be53-0bf8552cbe2c - New Guy term
// 3702ae2e-9861-42b6-b67d-a2fecf222405 - StarWars term
ctx.DataProvider.get_properties()["UserSegmentTerms"] = ['b34abf38-d746-4037-be53-0bf8552cbe2c','3702ae2e-9861-42b6-b67d-a2fecf222405'];
```

This will make the next search executed on the search page trigger promoted result as the term GUID's is passed along with the query, triggering the promoted result query rule.

Summary

To recap, using business rules and query rules you assembled a user context to show promoted result for users who are new employees and who also like *StarWars*. How you implement to define what a new guy is and if a person likes *StarWars* or not, that's entirely up to you, and the hardest part of the equation for sure.

If you managed to master the art of user contexts combined with query rules there is no doubt you can achieve greatness for your users. If you're lucky you might even get some fame :-)

References

Set up User Segmentation to drive adaptive experiences in a Product Catalog in SharePoint 2013
http://blogs.msdn.com/b/adaptive_experiences_in_sharepoint_2013/archive/2012/11/14/set-up-user-segmentation-to-drive-adaptive-experiences-in-a-product-catalog-in-sharepoint-2013.aspx

Managing Search Relevance in SharePoint 2013 and O365
http://channel9.msdn.com/Events/SharePoint-Conference/2014/SPC382

github.com/SPCSR - Search control template which set's user segment based on Department
http://bit.ly/1zZ397a

Inconvenient Content Targeting with User Segments in Search REST API
http://blog.mastykarz.nl/inconvenient-content-targeting-user-segments-search-rest-api/

SharePoint 2013 No Code User Segment Search
http://blogs.technet.com/b/peter_dempsey/archive/2014/03/24/sharepoint-2013-no-code-user-segment-search.aspx

MSDN: User segmentation in SharePoint 2013
http://msdn.microsoft.com/en-us/library/office/jj870831(v=office.15).aspx

Chapter 10

Search Orchestration

This chapter cover two main objectives. Firstly how to configure search for any page to make it manageable in the long run, and secondly how to configure search for that same page to make the page show as fast as possible to the end-user.

The main tool used to accomplish this is *Result Block Routing* in a *Query Rule*. If you haven't read about it before, now is certainly the time.

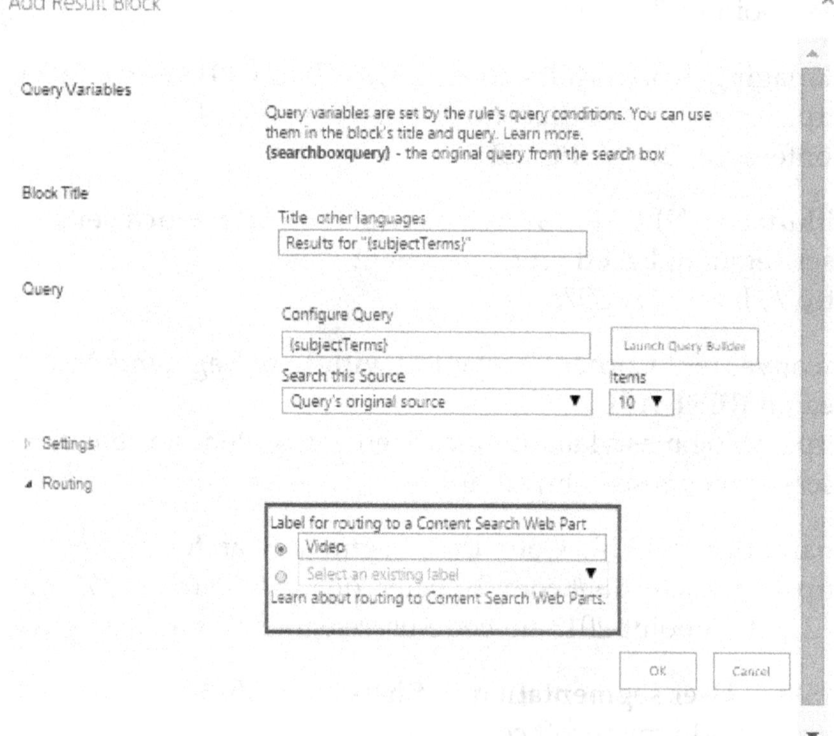

When designing intranet's in SharePoint Online/2013 the front page is often driven by a lot of Content Search Web Parts, and you quickly end up with 4+ parts on your page.

A typical layout could look something like the image below with seven sections, all driven by search.

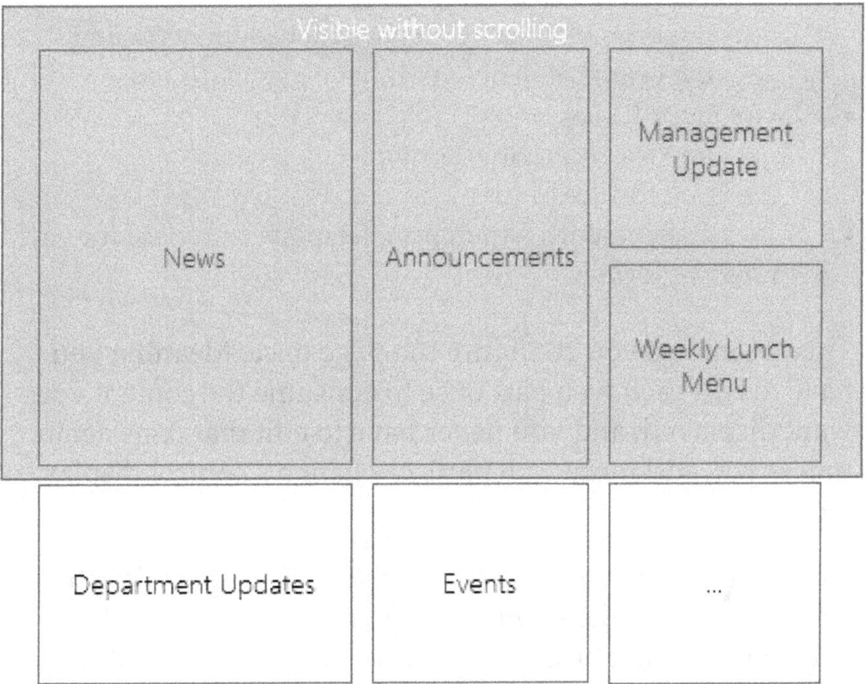

If you look at the layout above the highlighted area in blue is what is above the fold, meaning what is visible before a user have to start scrolling. In the design there are four web parts visible right away, and three which are not visible.

Every search query executed will consume server time, and will impact how quickly data is brought back to the browser. If you load up more data than needed, your end-user gets penalized and have to wait longer until the page is displayed.

Ideally you would configure the page the following way:

- Nine Result Sources
    - one for each section
    - one for triggering the visible content
    - one for triggering the hidden content
- Seven Content Search Web Parts
    - the ones visible will have synchronous loading
    - the ones not visible will have asynchronous loading
- Two Query Rules
    - one for the visible content
    - one for the hidden content
- A Result Type with a matching Display Template for each rendering format

This set-up lets you configure the page once. Meaning you have to edit each web part once to consume the content you want displayed, and you never have to edit that page again, unless you add more web parts or change a control display template.

Any change to what you want to show on the page is achieved by either editing the *Result Sources* or the *Query Rules*. See Chapter 4 for more information and the importance of using *Result Sources*.

As an example let's use the Contoso demo site which can be set up using *www.microsoftofficedemos.com* (if you are a Microsoft Partner).The red squares highlights the search web parts, and as you can see, there is only one search area which is visible upon first loading of the page. You will leave this web part as is, and orchestrate the last four with a query rule.

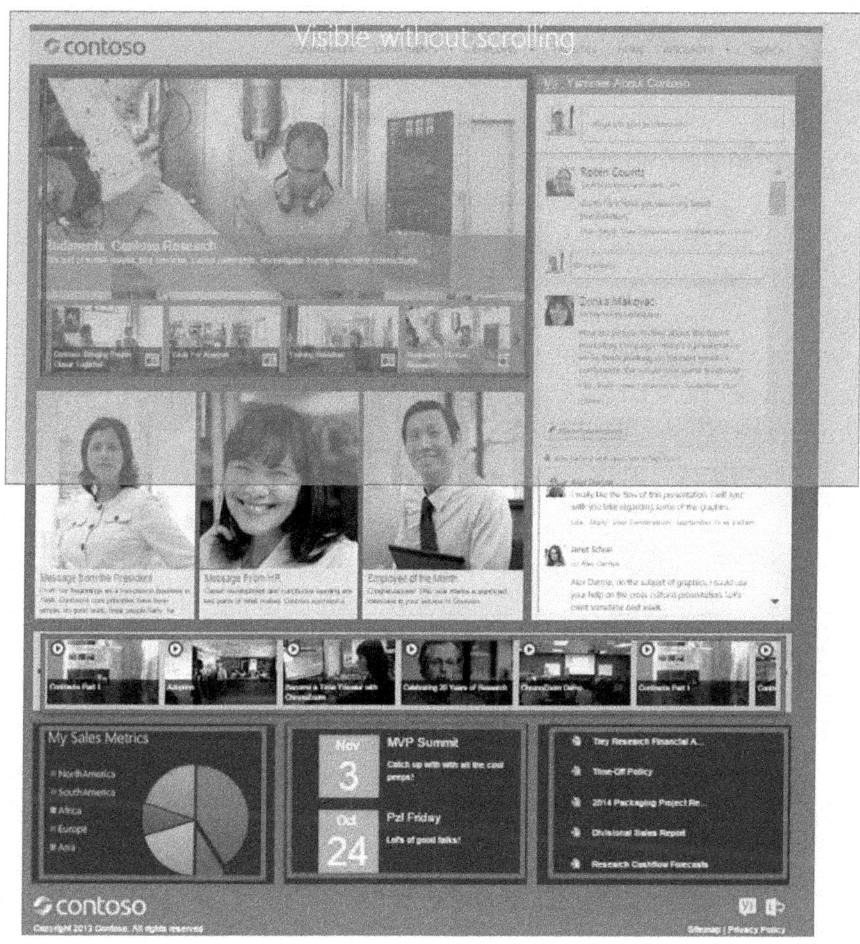

The following steps are required for the optimization/orchestration:

- Create an empty result source with no query in it, which will act as the trigger source for your orchestrating query rule
- Create a query rule triggered by the above result source
  - Hard code the queries in the rule and not create separate result sources for this demo
- Add four result blocks to the rule, and give each one a routing name
- Configure the four content search web parts at the bottom of the page to be asynchronous and consume the routed content

Any search web part configured to load data synchronously, will have the search results as part of the HTML upon page load (as JSON objects). This is the default behavior of the CSWP.

The Empty Result Source

Create a new *Result Source* named *Lazy Loader*, and remove the query transformation.

General Information

Names must be unique at each administrative level. For example, two result sources in a site cannot share a name, but one in a site and one provided by the site collection can.

Descriptions are shown as tooltips when selecting result sources in other configuration pages.

Name

Lazy Loader

Description

Protocol

Select Local SharePoint for results from the index of this Search Service.

Select OpenSearch 1.0/1.1 for results from a search engine that uses that protocol.

Select Exchange for results from an exchange source.

Select Remote SharePoint for results from the index of a search service hosted in another farm.

- (•) Local SharePoint
- ( ) Remote SharePoint
- ( ) OpenSearch 1.0/1.1
- ( ) Exchange

Type

Select SharePoint Search Results to search over the entire index.

Select People Search Results to enable query processing specific to People Search, such as phonetic name matching or nickname matching. Only people profiles will be returned from a People Search source.

- (•) SharePoint Search Results
- ( ) People Search Results

Query Transform

Change incoming queries to use this new query text instead. Include the incoming query in the new text by using the query variable "{searchTerms}".

Launch Query Builder

The Query Rule

I've created a rule named *Below The Fold,* with four result blocks. Each block has been configured with the amount of results to return. 10 for video's which is the max in a block, two for events, five for documents and one for BI.

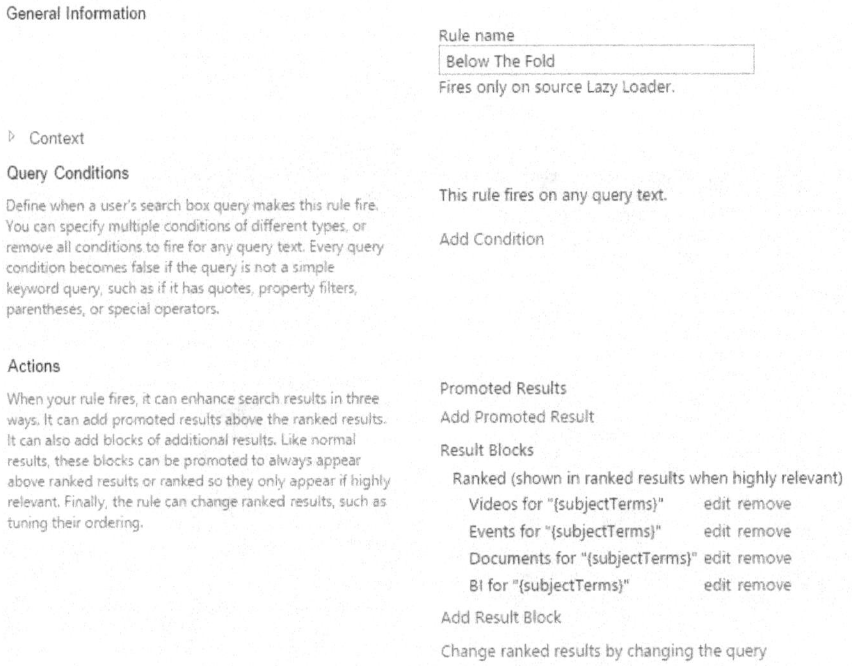

General Information

Rule name

Below The Fold

Fires only on source Lazy Loader.

▷ Context

Query Conditions

Define when a user's search box query makes this rule fire. You can specify multiple conditions of different types, or remove all conditions to fire for any query text. Every query condition becomes false if the query is not a simple keyword query, such as if it has quotes, property filters, parentheses, or special operators.

This rule fires on any query text.

Add Condition

Actions

When your rule fires, it can enhance search results in three ways. It can add promoted results above the ranked results. It can also add blocks of additional results. Like normal results, these blocks can be promoted to always appear above ranked results or ranked so they only appear if highly relevant. Finally, the rule can change ranked results, such as tuning their ordering.

Promoted Results

Add Promoted Result

Result Blocks

Ranked (shown in ranked results when highly relevant)

Videos for "{subjectTerms}" edit remove

Events for "{subjectTerms}" edit remove

Documents for "{subjectTerms}" edit remove

BI for "{subjectTerms}" edit remove

Add Result Block

Change ranked results by changing the query

Web Part Configuration

First, edit the video carousel web part, and click *Change Query*. When you pick *Lazy Loader* as the source, the preview to the right shows items grouped per the routing names.

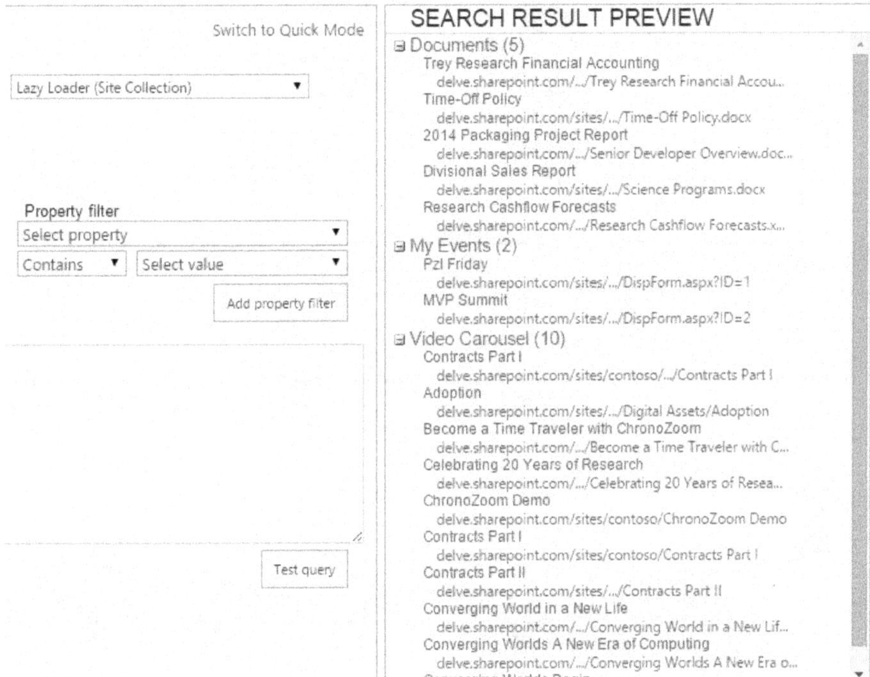

Go over to the *SETTINGS* tab, and make the web part load results asynchronously.

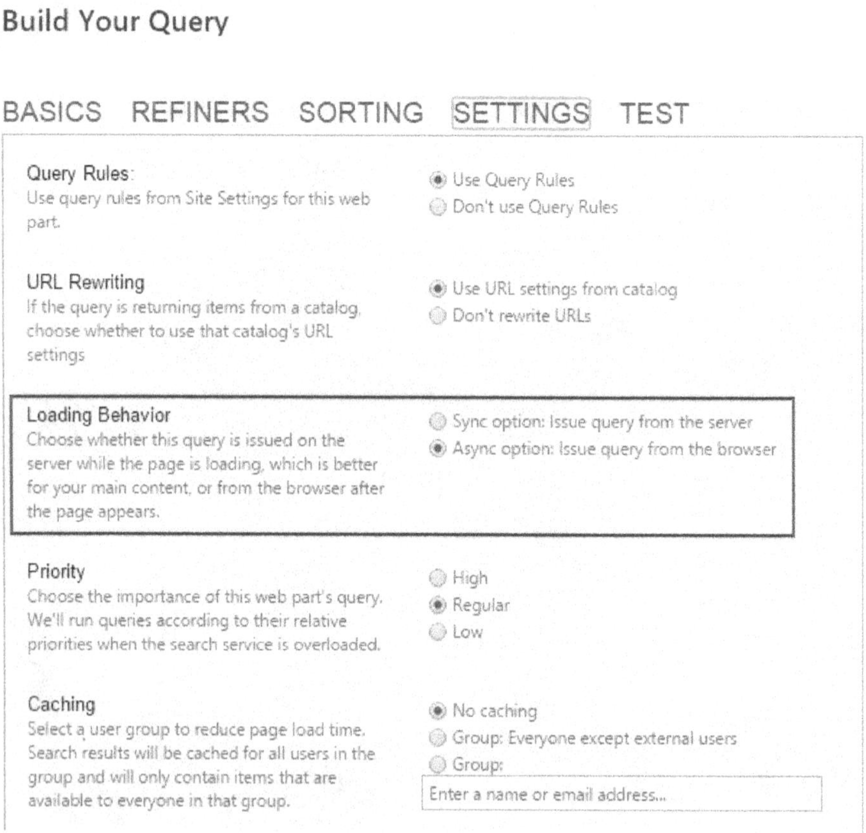

Build Your Query

BASICS REFINERS SORTING SETTINGS TEST

Query Rules:
Use query rules from Site Settings for this web part.

- (•) Use Query Rules
- ( ) Don't use Query Rules

URL Rewriting
If the query is returning items from a catalog, choose whether to use that catalog's URL settings

- (•) Use URL settings from catalog
- ( ) Don't rewrite URLs

Loading Behavior
Choose whether this query is issued on the server while the page is loading, which is better for your main content, or from the browser after the page appears.

- ( ) Sync option: Issue query from the server
- (•) Async option: Issue query from the browser

Priority
Choose the importance of this web part's query. We'll run queries according to their relative priorities when the search service is overloaded.

- ( ) High
- (•) Regular
- ( ) Low

Caching
Select a user group to reduce page load time. Search results will be cached for all users in the group and will only contain items that are available to everyone in that group.

- (•) No caching
- ( ) Group: Everyone except external users
- ( ) Group:

Enter a name or email address...

Save your query settings, expand the *Settings* section for the web part properties, and pick *Video Carousel* from the list in *Result Tables*. *RelevantResults* is the default table which usually carries your results, and *RefinementResults* has any refiners configured, in case you've skipped this configuration part when you have previously used the CSWP.

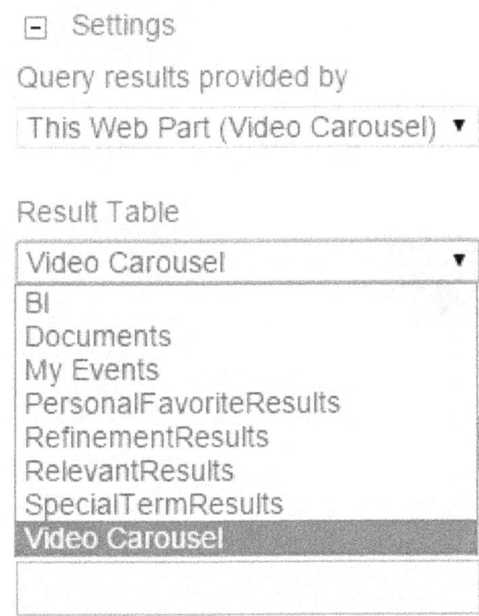

For the other search web parts set the asynchronous setting from the Query Builder, ignore the source location, expand the properties for the web part, select results to be provided by the *Video Carousel* web part, and choose the appropriate routing table for your web part. Now you're seeing where we are going with the whole routing part. One web part retrieves all the result and passes them on to the other web parts.

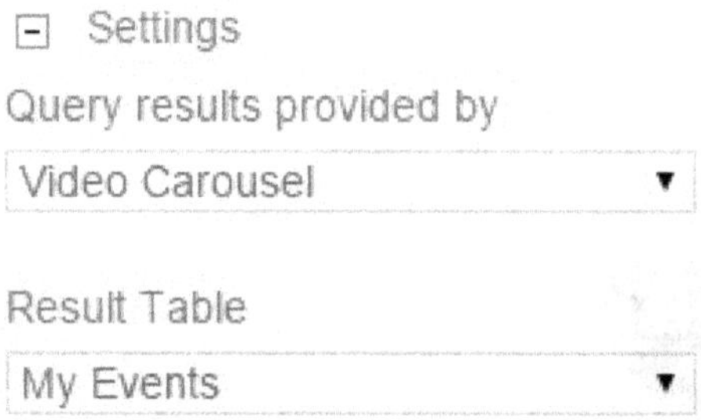

Settings

Query results provided by

Video Carousel

Result Table

My Events

In page edit mode you can see information stating the web part is consuming results from another web part.

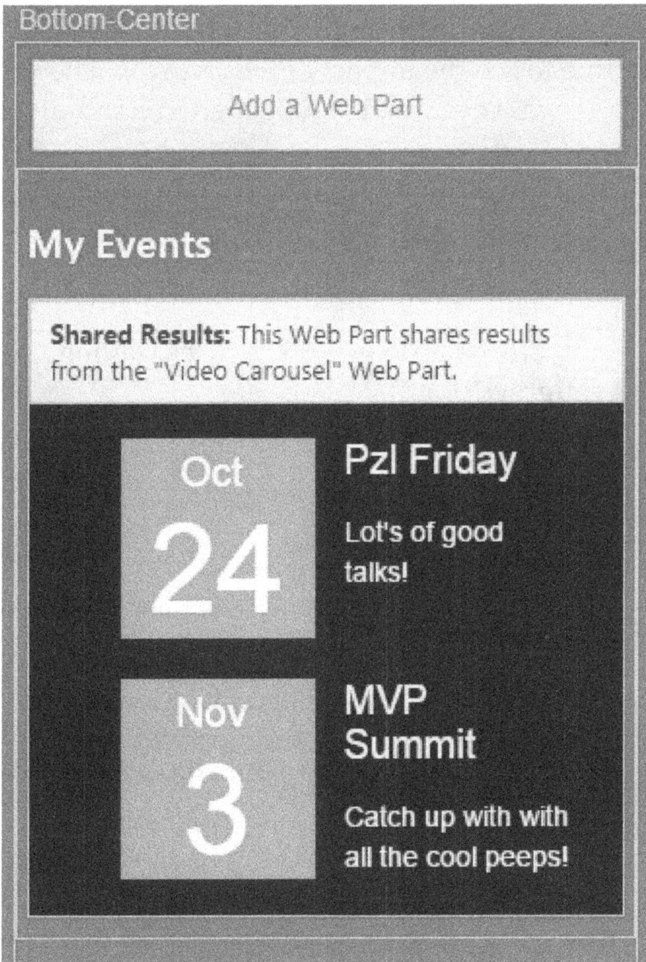

Summary - Default vs. Optimized/Orchestrated

Now that you've been jumping through hoops and following my direction, it's time to see the impact of the changes. The measurements below was captured used the network monitor in Chrome.

Page Size	
Un-optimized	186.262 bytes
Optimized	135.218 + 41.515 = 176.733 bytes (saving roughly 10k)
Time to DOM Content Loaded event *10 samples – not scientific*	
Un-optimized	2 seconds
Optimized	1.5 seconds

So for this one-user test case, you save 10kb of bandwidth and half a second before the page is shown. And you will save a whole lot of time when you want to change the filter or sort logic of one of the result blocks. You can simply change the query for the corresponding result block without checking out the page.

Most likely the biggest benefit is for you as a search orchestrator to save time setting up the page initially, with a potential added benefit for the end-user regarding response time for the page.

References

Workaround to show Contact items in People Search
http:\techmikael.blogspot.com\2014\04\workaround-to-show-contact-items-in.html

Create query rules for web content management in SharePoint Server 2013
http://technet.microsoft.com/en-us/library/jj871014(v=office.15).aspx#BKMK_ConfigureContentSearchWP

Chapter 11

FAST Query Language (FQL)

The first two chapters covered KQL and a couple of the new operators introduced with SharePoint 2013 which came from FQL - XRANK, NEAR and ONEAR.
In addition FQL has even more operators, some of them listed below:

- starts-with
- ends-width
- count
- andnot
- range

Note: There are also other operators which gives you great control over how a query is being sent over and parsed, and I recommend reading over the samples at FAST Query Language (FQL) syntax reference.

FQL is sort of hidden away in SharePoint and no one really talks about it, while at the same time the underlying search engine (and the refiner UI) in SharePoint (still) uses FQL.

This means KQL statements are translated to FQL before being executed. If this will hold true forever no one knows. But until the FQL part of the search engine is being rewritten at some point in the future, if ever, it will stay. And it is also very well documented at MSDN. For search developers this is good news as FQL has some tricks up it sleeve compared to the polished KQL counterpart.

Syntax

A notable difference between KQL and FQL is the query syntax. Where KQL typically writes

exp OPERATOR exp OPERATOR exp

FQL uses a nested syntax

OPERATOR(OPERATOR(EXP,EXP),OPERATOR(EXP,EXP))

Operators can also be combined in different ways, and you may achieve the same result with different ways of writing a query.

KQL	***foo OR bar***
FQL	or(foo,bar)
FQL	string("foo bar", mode="or")

KQL	**title="foo bar" title="zoo animal"**
FQL	or(title:equals("foo bar"),title:equals("zoo animal"))
FQL	title:equals(or("foo bar","zoo animal"))

KQL	**id=1 id=3 id=4 id=10 id=12**
FQL	id:int("1 3 4 10 12", mode="or")

Personally the FQL operators I find most useful are *starts-with* and *ends-with* which can be used to find matching terms at the start and end of a field. **You cannot do wildcard matches with starts-with/ends-with, only term based matching.** KQL supports equals (=) and contains (:), but no matching at the start or end. You would typically use this against a managed property like a phone number. 555-1234

- phonenumber:starts-with("555")
- phonenumber:ends-with("1234")

Query on dates

Another useful scenario is when you want to filter on dates with a higher resolution than day. KQL will disregard any time portion of a date query while FQL will honor it. The sample below will return all documents produced after 12:35:57GMT.

write:range(2014-12-15T12:35:57.0000000Z,max,from="gt")

Querying using FQL

If you want to run a query using FQL you either have to use an FQL enables result source, where you on your REST or SSOM query set ENABLEFQL to true. This is not possible using CSOM today.

The easier and perhaps better alternative is to write your FQL statements as refinement filters. Refiner statements are by default sent over as FQL filters and enables a very powerful query feature by combining KQL and FQL in the same query. Note that FQL sent in the refinement part will not be part of the ranked expression - except with explicit XRANK statements.

Summary

If you ever find a scenario where KQL just don't cut it, then take look at FQL and see if it provides the missing functionality you are looking for.

References

FAST Query Language (FQL) syntax reference
http://msdn.microsoft.com/en-us/library/office/ff394606%28v=office.15%29.aspx

Limiting search results by exact time in SharePoint 2013–and how to do FQL
http://techmikael.blogspot.com/2013/07/limiting-search-results-by-exact-time.html

Appending query terms in SharePoint 2013/O365 without adding them to the search box
http://techmikael.blogspot.com/2013/09/appending-query-terms-in-sharepoint.html

DateTime resolution for querying FAST for SharePoint
http://techmikael.blogspot.com/2011/04/datetime-resolution-for-querying-fast.html

Building search queries in SharePoint 2013 (FQL enabled Result Source)
http://msdn.microsoft.com/en-us/library/office/jj163973(v=office.15).aspx

Bonus Chapter

Content Search Web Part vs. Search Results Web Part

If you have an Enterprise license for SharePoint 2013 on-premises or you are using SharePoint Online Plan 2 (Office 365 E3/E4) then you have both web parts available. If you don't have the E powers (e-CAL licenses), you only have the Search Result Web Part. In what scenarios can you use the Search Result Web Part when you don't have the license for CSWP and still deliver excellent search driven solutions?

The table below list functionality and differences between the web parts. Some search result query specific functionality is omitted like language dropdown, sorting and preferences, as they are more relevant to an interactive search page, and not a search driven page.

Feature	**CSWP**	**Search Result WP**
Property Mappings via web part settings	X	
Start displaying results from specified result number	via web part settings or #s= URL parameter	via the *s*= URL parameter
Don't show anything if there are no results	X	via custom control template
Caching support	X	

Support content routing, choosing result table	X	
Support paging	Via "List with Paging" control template	Via web part settings
Choose display template based on Result Type		X
Manually choose display template for all items	X	X
Refine/filter results	with query builder or URL parameter	with query builder or URL parameter
Support async/sync first load	X	X
Support include duplicates	X	X
Support query rules	X	X
Use catalog URL instead of real URL	X	X
Max # of results to show (without hack)	50	50

Show promoted results	via result table	via control / display template

In general, any URL parameter you can use with the Search Result web part you can also use with the CSWP.

Summary

As you see from the above table, the two web parts overlap on almost all parts of functionality. The CSWP has some more web property settings making it easier to use without editing display templates directly, it support caching which is useful for publishing scenarios where a lot of people have the same read access to the items displayed, and lastly it allows content orchestration which was covered in Chapter 10, allowing better workflows and page loading optimizations when constructing search driven pages.

References

How to enable Content Search Web Part Display Templates for Search Result Web Part
http://techmikael.blogspot.com/2014/12/how-to-enable-content-search-web-part.html

www.ingramcontent.com/pod-product-compliance
Lightning Source LLC
Chambersburg PA
CBHW071005050326
40689CB00014B/3502
9781505887037